Excel
Get the Results You Want!

Years 5–6
Selective Schools Thinking Skills Tests

Lyn Baker, Sharon Dalgleish, Tanya Dalgleish & Hamish McLean

PASCAL PRESS

© 2023 Lyn Baker, Sharon Dalgleish, Tanya Dalgleish, Hamish McLean and Pascal Press

Completely new edition incorporating late 2020 Selective School test changes

Reprinted 2024

ISBN 978 1 74125 633 8

Pascal Press Pty Ltd
PO Box 250
Glebe NSW 2037
(02) 9198 1748
www.pascalpress.com.au

Publisher: Vivienne Joannou
Project editor: Mark Dixon
Edited by Mark Dixon and Rosemary Peers
Answers checked by Dale Little and Peter Little
Cover by DiZign Pty Ltd
Typeset by Grizzly Graphics (Leanne Richters)
Printed by Vivar Printing/Green Giant Press

Contents

Practice questions

Sample tests

Answers

ABOUT THIS BOOK

The tests in this book help you prepare to undertake the Thinking Skills question paper of the Selective High School Placement Test. The Thinking Skills Test assesses your ability to:

- problem solve
- think critically and logically
- judge whether a conclusion must be true or cannot be true
- analyse an argument for flaws in reasoning or correct reasoning
- judge whether additional evidence supports or weakens an argument
- compare and order objects and information
- solve puzzles involving numbers, shapes and measurements
- analyse and interpret information contained in graphs and diagrams.

ABOUT THE SELECTIVE SCHOOL TEST

The NSW Selective High School Placement Test consists of four sections:

- **Reading** (30 questions in 40 minutes)
- **Thinking Skills** (40 questions in 40 minutes)
- **Mathematical Reasoning** (35 questions in 40 minutes)
- **Writing** (one question in 30 minutes).

The tests, except Writing, are in multiple-choice form, with each question being of equal value. Marks are awarded for each correct answer and applicants are advised to guess the answer if they are uncertain.

HOW THE RESULTS ARE USED BY PUBLIC SCHOOLS

Entry to selective high schools is based on academic merit. In 2022 changes were made to the allocation of places. Under the Equity Placement Model, up to 20% of places are held for members of the following disadvantaged and under-represented groups:

- students from low socio-educational advantage backgrounds
- First Nations students
- rural and remote students
- students with disability.

It is important to remember that the places allocated under the Equity Placement Model will not necessarily be filled. In 2023, the first year of this new system, less than 10% of these places were offered. This means that more than 90% of the places were offered to general applicants. The new system has helped close the educational gap in participation from disadvantaged groups without having a significant impact on other applicants.

Students no longer receive a test score or placement rank. The new performance report will instead place students in one of the following categories:

- top 10% of candidates
- next 15% of candidates
- next 25% of candidates
- lowest 50% of candidates.

This change addresses privacy and wellbeing concerns including unhealthy competition between students. The sole purpose of the test is to identify students who would benefit from the chance to study at a selective school and, since it doesn't test knowledge of the curriculum, there is no diagnostic merit in the test—unlike the NAPLAN test, which can help identify areas where children can improve.

Minimum entry scores for selective schools are no longer published because these change from year to year and depend on the number of applicants, their relative performance and the number of families who decline an offer. Students placed on the reserve list no longer receive a numerical rank; instead an indication of how long it will take to receive an offer, based on previous years, is provided.

A selection committee for each selective high school decides which students are to be offered places. These committees also decide how many students are to be placed on the reserve list. Should a student with a confirmed offer turn down a place at a selective school, the place will be offered to the first student on the reserve list.

There is an appeals panel for illness or other mitigating circumstances. All applicants are advised of the outcome. The NSW Government provides detailed information on the application and selection process for parents on the Selective High School Placement Test. This is available from: https://education.nsw. gov.au/parents-and-carers/learning/tests-and-exams/selective-school-test.

Sample test papers are also available on this website.

ADVICE TO STUDENTS

The tests are difficult and you may not finish them in the time available. Don't worry about this because many students will also find the questions very hard. You can't learn the answers to the questions in these tests like you can with some school tests because they force you to deal with new situations.

Here is a summary of the advice the NSW Education Department gives to people taking the tests:

- There is nothing special that you have to learn in order to do these tests.
- These are tests to see whether you can think clearly with words and numbers.

- Listen carefully to the instructions.
- If you are not sure what to do then ask.
- Make sure you know where to mark the answers for each test.
- Do not open the test booklet until you are told.
- Read each question carefully before giving your answer.
- There is no penalty for guessing—so guess if you are not sure.
- Don't rush—work steadily and as carefully as you can.
- If a question is too hard, don't worry— come back to it later if you have time.
- It is easy to get your answers out of order so always check the number of the question you are answering.
- Every now and then make sure the answer is in the correctly numbered circle.
- Feel free to write on the question booklet for any rough working.
- Don't do any rough work on the answer sheet.
- If you want to change an answer, rub it out and fill in the appropriate circle for your new answer.
- Keep track of the time—you will not be told when time is running out.
- Don't fold the answer sheet—it has to be put through a machine to mark it.

Thinking Skills answer sheet

Mark your answers here.

To answer each question, fill in the appropriate circle for your chosen answer.

Use a pencil. If you make a mistake or change your mind, erase and try again.

You can make extra copies of this answer sheet to mark your answers to the Sample Thinking Skills Tests in this book.

	A B C D		A B C D		A B C D		A B C D
1	○○○○	11	○○○○	21	○○○○	31	○○○○
2	○○○○	12	○○○○	22	○○○○	32	○○○○
3	○○○○	13	○○○○	23	○○○○	33	○○○○
4	○○○○	14	○○○○	24	○○○○	34	○○○○
5	○○○○	15	○○○○	25	○○○○	35	○○○○
6	○○○○	16	○○○○	26	○○○○	36	○○○○
7	○○○○	17	○○○○	27	○○○○	37	○○○○
8	○○○○	18	○○○○	28	○○○○	38	○○○○
9	○○○○	19	○○○○	29	○○○○	39	○○○○
10	○○○○	20	○○○○	30	○○○○	40	○○○○

Practice questions

1 Whoever ate Baby Bear's porridge must have had both an opportunity and a motive.

If this is true, which one of these sentences **cannot** be true?

A If Goldilocks ate Baby Bear's porridge, she would have had a motive.

B If Goldilocks did not eat Baby Bear's porridge, she cannot have had an opportunity.

C If Goldilocks did not have a motive, she cannot have been the one to eat Baby Bear's porridge.

D If Goldilocks did not have an opportunity to eat the porridge, she must have been the one to eat it.

2 Koalas are officially listed as an endangered species along the east coast of Australia. Their biggest threat is loss of habitat caused by tree clearing. The more time koalas spend on the ground walking longer distances to new trees, the greater their risk from dogs and cars. Climate change is also impacting the koala's chance of survival because of bushfires and floods.

Send a message to key politicians to act now to reduce climate change and prevent further land clearing to save koalas from extinction.

Which one of these statements, if true, most **strengthens** the above argument?

A The government should provide money to save koalas.

B Droughts and high temperatures are negatively impacting koalas.

C Drive slowly at night because koalas are nocturnal.

D Join a local volunteer group to plant koala food trees in your neighbourhood.

3 There are two ways to qualify for the regional athletics championships: by winning three school-based events, such as shot-put, discus and javelin, or by breaking a regional record.

This year eight students from Lana's school have qualified for the regional athletics championships.

Lana: 'I know five regional records were broken by students at our school this year. So that means three of our qualifiers must have won three school-based events.'

Which one of the following sentences shows the mistake Lana has made?

A Some regional records may have been broken in previous years.

B The number of regional records broken this year may be higher than usual.

C Some students who broke a regional record may also have won three or more school events.

D Some of the students from Lana's school may have broken more than one record.

Practice questions

4 The following is one piece of a 3D puzzle.

Which of the pieces below fits with the piece above to make a cube? The pieces may be rotated.

A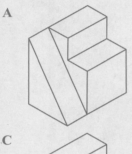

B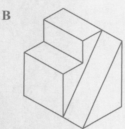

C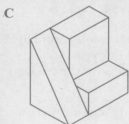

D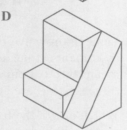

5 Two cyclists compete in a race that involves completing 18 laps of a circuit. The cyclists ride at a constant speed and Jan completes three laps in the same time it takes Niils to complete four laps.

If the race starts at 9 am and Niils completes the race at 10:30 am, at what time does Jan complete the race?

A 10 am   B 10:45 am
C 11 am   D 11:30 am

6 Gilbert, Kelly, Mel, Pia and Leonard are seated around a circular table with six seats.

- Gilbert is directly opposite the empty seat.
- Kelly is not sitting next to Gilbert.
- Mel is two spaces away from Pia.

A sixth friend Bridgitte sits down in the empty seat. Who is she sitting next to?

A Mel and Leonard
B Mel and Kelly
C Kelly and Pia
D Kelly and Leonard

Answers to practice questions

1 **D is correct.** This option does not make sense. If opportunity and motive are required and Goldilocks did not have an opportunity, she cannot have been the one to eat the porridge.

The other options are incorrect. These answers could each be true.

2 **B is correct.** The argument is that politicians need to act to save koalas from extinction. This argument is supported by evidence that tree clearing and climate change are threats to koalas. This statement strengthens the argument by adding the threat to koalas caused by droughts and high temperatures.

A is incorrect. This statement doesn't strengthen the argument.

C and D are incorrect. These statements do not support the argument that politicians need to act now.

3 **C is correct.** Lana has assumed that, because five regional records were broken by students at the school this year, there were three students who qualified for the regionals by winning three school-based events. However, it may be that some students broke a regional record and also won school-based events.

A and B are incorrect. These sentences could be true but they are irrelevant to Lana's mistake.

D is incorrect. This sentence could be true but it is not the mistake Lana has made, as she didn't think of this in her response.

4 **B is correct.** It can be useful to think of rotating each piece on a skewer to see where it fits. If the solid from B is looked at from another side, and then rotated around the skewer shown, we can picture it fitting with the original piece.

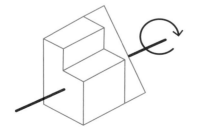 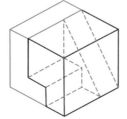

A more methodical approach is to look at the features of the possible piece. The bottom level of the solid must be 2 layers high to fit with the first piece.

C and D are therefore incorrect as the bottom level is only 1 layer high.

By looking at the side of the sloped section we can see the answer must be B.

5 **C is correct.** Niils completes the race of 18 laps in 1 hour and 30 minutes. So he rides 6 laps in half an hour and 12 laps in an hour.

If Jan completes 3 laps for every 4 that Niils rides, he will only complete 9 laps when Niils completes 12 laps. That is, he will ride 9 laps every hour.

So it will take Jan 2 hours to complete the race as 9 laps × 2 = 18 laps.

He will finish 2 hours after 9 am at 11 am.

6 **D is correct.** Gilbert is sitting opposite the empty seat. Kelly must be sitting on one side of the empty seat as she cannot be seated next to Gilbert.

If Mel is two spaces from Pia, she cannot be next to the empty seat as she will then be exactly 2 seats away from Kelly and from Gilbert, not Pia. So Mel must be next to Gilbert and Pia must be next to Gilbert on his other side.

One possible arrangement is shown here. Note that the positions of Mel and Pia can be swapped, as can the positions of Kelly and Leonard.

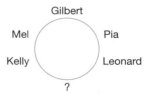

Kelly and Leonard occupy the seats next to the empty seat which Bridgitte is to sit in.

SAMPLE TEST 1

1 Five calves, Bluebell, Buttercup, Daisy, Pansy and Poppy, are all in a paddock. Daisy is 1 week younger than Poppy. Buttercup and Pansy were born on the same day. Bluebell is 4 weeks older than Daisy. Pansy is 2 weeks older than Poppy.

Only one of the following sentences is **not** true. Which is it?

A Buttercup is 2 weeks younger than Bluebell.

B Buttercup is 3 weeks older than Daisy.

C Bluebell is the oldest.

D Daisy is the youngest.

2 If Heike argues with her mother once more this week, she will definitely not be allowed to visit her friends on Saturday.

If she can't visit her friends on Saturday, she will miss out on planning for Gabi's birthday celebration.

If Heike can get through the rest of the week without arguing with her mother, she might be allowed to visit her friends and be able to help plan Gabi's party.

Which one of the following outcomes is **not** possible?

A Heike argued with her mother and was not permitted to visit her friends.

B Heike did not argue with her mother but was still not allowed to visit her friends.

C Heike was allowed to visit her friends and helped plan the birthday celebration.

D Heike was not allowed to visit her friends on Saturday but still helped plan for the party.

3 Alice, Cara, Jess, Paige, Susie and Victoria sit at a round table. Alice sits opposite Cara.

Susie is on Jess's right and Jess is opposite Paige who is next to Alice.

Who sits on Cara's immediate left?

A Jess   B Susie

C Paige   D Victoria

4 A group of 5 adults and 6 children are going to the circus. The children are aged 13, 11, 9, 7, 5 and 3. The ticket prices are:

TICKET PRICES

Adults and children over 12 (single ticket): $10.00

Couple (any two people together): $15.00

Family (any four people together): $25.00

Children under 5: Free

Children aged 5 to 12: Half adult single price

What is the lowest price the group can pay?

A $52.50   B $60   C $62.50   D $65

5 The Australian sea lion is one of the rarest sea-lion species in the world. Numbers of this sea lion have dropped dramatically in the recent past. The biggest threat to the survival of the species is commercial fishing which uses gillnets. The sea lions get caught and trapped in the gillnets and drown. Commercial fishing should not be allowed near sea-lion colonies.

Which of these statements, if true, most **strengthens** the above argument?

A Accurate population monitoring is needed to ensure the sea-lion population does not decline further.

B Numbers of sea-lion pups born each year are declining.

C Fishing companies need to be held accountable for their impact on sea-lion colonies.

D Gillnets can entangle other ocean species including dolphins, turtles and sharks.

SAMPLE TEST 1

6 A local drama society is staging a play. The play will open on 4 June and the final performance will be on 27 June. The play will be staged every night of the week except for Monday. There will be an extra afternoon production every Saturday and a special charity performance on the afternoon of Sunday 13 June. How many times will the play be performed?

   A 23   **B** 24   **C** 25   **D** 26

7 The top has been torn from this sum of three two-digit numbers.

$$\begin{array}{r} +92 \\ \hline 178 \end{array}$$

Gabriel knows that no digit was repeated, so only one of the 10 digits was not used.

Which digit did **not** appear in the sum?

   A 3   **B** 4   **C** 5   **D** 6

8 The notice for the school concert advised as follows:

> Raffle tickets will be available for purchase at $5 each or three tickets for $10. There are five fantastic prizes to win. There will also be a lucky door prize. A ticket for the lucky door prize will be given to each attendee on entry to the concert hall. Prize winners will be announced at the end of the concert.

Grace: 'Six people will be prize winners on the night.'

Which one of the following sentences shows the mistake Grace has made?

   A Some people might not buy any raffle tickets.

   B Any one person could win a number of raffle prizes as well as the lucky door prize.

   C The school might not draw the raffle on the night if they don't sell enough tickets.

   D There are six prizes to win on the night.

9 'Someone has stolen Ben's T-shirts off the clothesline behind the unit block. Whoever stole them must have had both an opportunity and a motive.'

If this is true, which one of these sentences must also be true?

   A If Noel did not steal the T-shirts, he cannot have had a motive.

   B If Noel had an opportunity, he must have stolen the T-shirts.

   C If Noel stole the T-shirts, he cannot have had a motive.

   D If Noel had a motive, he cannot have stolen the T-shirts.

10 A piece of a three-dimensional puzzle is shown below:

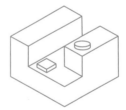

Which piece below will fit with the piece above to make a cube?

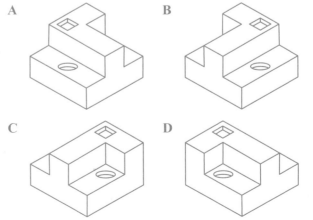

   A   B

   C   D

☞ **Answers and explanations on pages 56–62**

11 At the end of term Ms Ellis, the dance teacher, gives scores for performance and attitude to each student in her dance class. These scores are added to give each student an overall score for dance. Last term Jack and Flynn got the same overall score.

Jack: 'If we got different scores for attitude, our scores in performance must have been different too.'

Flynn: 'And if our scores for attitude were the same, our scores in performance must have been the same too.'

If the information in the box is true, whose reasoning is correct?

A Jack only

B Flynn only

C Both Jack and Flynn

D Neither Jack nor Flynn

12 Bella's school was selecting students to attend a leadership conference. Students could nominate themselves to attend or they could be nominated by a teacher. Once nominated, a student then had to complete a school-service challenge as well as an interview with the Principal.

If a student was nominated by a teacher, then they only had to pass the school-service challenge in order to be selected to attend. If a student was not nominated by a teacher, then they either needed an excellent result in the school-service challenge or they needed to do well in both the school-service challenge and the interview.

Bella was nominated by a teacher but failed to be selected to attend the leadership conference. What must have been the reason?

A She did badly in the interview.

B She was not nominated by a teacher.

C She failed the school-service challenge.

D She did well in the school-service challenge but badly in the interview.

13 Four friends are riding the four bikes pictured. The smaller wheels are the same size and the larger wheels are the same size. Terrence is riding bike 1. Gloria is riding bike 2. Celeste is riding bike 3 and Louis is riding bike 4.

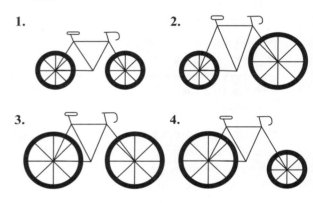

If the friends are riding in such a way that all the back wheels of the bikes make a full revolution in the exact same amount of time, which statement is **not** true?

A Gloria's front wheel is turning the fastest.

B Louis's front wheel is turning the fastest.

C Terrence and Gloria are moving at the same speed.

D Celeste and Louis are moving faster than the others.

14 The local Council was meeting to consider closing the Riverside Skate Park. Daisy, who regularly skateboards at the park, spoke at the meeting.

Daisy: 'We must keep Riverside Skate Park open. It is a much-needed safe place where young people from our area can hang out, have fun and make new friends—all while learning new skills and being physically active. It provides significant benefits for the whole community.'

Which one of these statements, if true, most **strengthens** Daisy's argument?

A Skate parks reduce illicit behaviour and damage to private property.

B A developer wants to buy the land to build an apartment block.

C A new Monster Skate Park is set to open in a nearby town next month.

D Young people feel safe hanging out at the Riverside Skate Park.

15 Dylan has a new car. His friend Hudson is reading the manual while Dylan drives. The manual says:

When the Tyre Pressure Warning Light on the dashboard comes on and stays on, it either means the air pressure is too low in at least one of the tyres or that there is a fault in the system.

Hudson: 'The Tyre Pressure Warning Light is not on now. So the pressure in all the tyres must be correct.'

Dylan: 'I checked the tyre pressure last week when I picked up the car so I know the tyres are all okay and the light won't come on.'

If the information in the box is true, whose reasoning is correct?

A Hudson only

B Dylan only

C Both Hudson and Dylan

D Neither Hudson nor Dylan

16 On a school camp, Sienna must choose four activities she would like to do. The timetable for the activities is below.

Session 1	Session 2
Kayaking	Basket weaving
Flying fox	Abseiling
Woodcarving	Flying fox
Orienteering	Obstacle course
Session 3	**Session 4**
Archery	High ropes
Woodcarving	Orienteering
Abseiling	Archery
Basket weaving	Obstacle course

If Sienna chooses High ropes, Archery and Woodcarving, which of the following is it **impossible** for her to choose?

A Abseiling

B Basket weaving

C Obstacle course

D Orienteering

17 **Pippa**: 'Let's go to the beach on Sunday.'

Leo: 'No, I can't. I have to study for the test on Monday. If I don't study, I'll probably fail.'

Pippa: 'If you fail the test, your parents won't be happy!'

Leo: 'Yes! If they are happy, I'm hoping they might let me go to Locky's party. But if they aren't happy, there is no way they'll let me go.'

Which one of the following outcomes is **not** possible?

A Leo did not study but his parents said yes to the party.

B Leo studied but his parents did not let him go to the party.

C Leo's parents were unhappy but they let him go to the party.

D Leo's parents were happy but they did not say yes to the party

18 Willow's dad entered a flower arrangement in a contest at the local community fair. In the contest, entrants are allowed to enter only one arrangement.

Dad: 'Judges score the arrangements and award ribbons for first, second and third. Plus there is also a ribbon for People's Choice.'

Willow: 'So that means four entrants will get ribbons!'

Which one of the following sentences shows the mistake Willow has made?

A One entrant might be awarded a ribbon for more than one arrangement.

B The People's Choice ribbon winner might also come first, second or third.

C Some arrangements might be disqualified.

D We don't know how many arrangements were entered in the contest.

19 Sports fans were surveyed and it was found that everyone who liked soccer also liked Aussie Rules. Some people who liked Aussie Rules also liked netball and all people who liked netball also liked rugby.

Hala was one of the fans surveyed. What **cannot** be true about Hala?

A She likes Aussie Rules but not soccer.

B She likes rugby but not Aussie Rules.

C She likes soccer but not Aussie Rules.

D She likes rugby but not soccer.

20 **Poppy**: 'My grandma always says 'waste not want not' when she saves the tiniest bit of leftover food.'

Whose reasoning is correct?

A **Ivy:** 'She means you'd better not waste your dinner now or you won't be hungry later.'

B **Emma:** 'It means if you use resources carefully, you will never be in need.'

C **Yorgos:** 'She means if you are wasteful, you will eventually have to go without food.'

D **Nick:** 'That expression means if you are not wasteful, then you will always want more things.'

☞ **Answers and explanations on pages 56–62**

21 'Whoever removed the fire extinguisher from the foyer wall must have had both an opportunity and a motive.'

If this is true, which one of these sentences must also be true?

A If Wan removed the fire extinguisher from the foyer wall, she cannot have had a motive.

B If Wan did not remove the fire extinguisher from the foyer wall, she must also have had an opportunity.

C If Wan did not have a motive, she cannot have removed the fire extinguisher from the foyer wall.

D If Wan had both a motive and an opportunity, she must have removed the fire extinguisher from the foyer wall.

22 Ajay and Quinn are on a bushwalk together. From their starting point the two friends walk along a track that goes 200 m north, 300 m west then 100 m north to a lookout. Once there they split up. Ajay walks back along the track they had just come on for 500 m. Quinn walks 100 m west, 200 m south, 200 m east and 100 m south.

Which option shows how far away and in what direction each person needs to go in order to return to the starting point?

A Ajay 100 m south, Quinn 200 m east

B Ajay 100 m north, Quinn 200 m west

C Ajay 100 m south, Quinn 200 m west

D Ajay 100 m north, Quinn 200 m east

23

> Creatures can be venomous or poisonous. An example of a venomous creature is a snake that bites its prey and injects it with toxin. An example of a poisonous creature is a cane toad, which has skin that is poisonous to touch or eat.'

If the information in the box is true, whose reasoning is **incorrect**?

A **Turvi**: 'An Asian tiger snake is poisonous and venomous because its bite injects deadly poison and it stores poison in its skin.'

B **Chanel**: 'The hairy-legged vampire bat is venomous. It preys on livestock animals by biting them.'

C **Georgie**: 'The hooded pitohui is a bird that has poisonous feathers and skin.'

D **Alan**: 'The Hawksbill sea turtle is venomous because it eats toxic algae and sponges and so its flesh becomes toxic. If you eat Hawksbill sea turtle, you can get symptoms of food poisoning.'

24 Seahorses are amazing fish but they face a grim future. Only one in 1000 live to more than six weeks of age. Some species are endangered due to destruction of their habitat from commercial fishing vessels, which trawl the sea floor and destroy the sponges and corals that provide food and shelter for seahorses. Over 150 million seahorses are caught each year worldwide. They are caught and dried for traditional Asian medicines and for sale as trinkets. Many are caught for the aquarium market.

Which one of the following, if true, most **strengthens** the above argument?

A Seahorses are sometimes caught as an unintended consequence of by-catch, especially by trawl fishers.

B Seahorse prospects will be improved by limiting fishing methods that create by-catch.

C Setting up marine protected areas where no commercial fishing is allowed will help seahorses survive.

D Banning trawl fishing will protect marine environments for all sea animals.

25 There are four towns:
- Town A is due north of Town C
- Town B is due north of Town D
- Town A is due west of Town B
- Town D is south-east of Town C.

What **cannot** be true about the distances between the towns?

A The distance between Town A and Town B is shorter than Town A to Town C.

B The distance between Town C and Town B is shorter than Town C to Town D.

C The distance between Town A and Town D is longer than Town C to Town B.

D The distance between Town A and Town C is longer than Town B to Town D.

26 These three pieces fit together to form the outside of a square. (They may need to be rotated.)

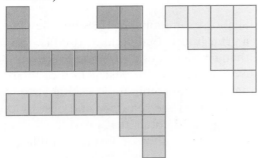

Which of these could be the inner piece of the square?

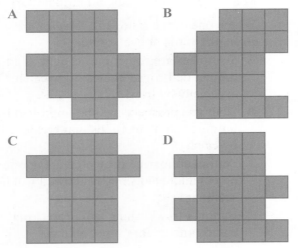

27 Abe, Bill, Dane, Farid and Vic each have an artwork hanging in the local gallery. The artworks are, in no particular order, a landscape, a seascape, a still life, a portrait and a photograph. They are all in a row on one wall of the art gallery.

- The portrait is on the far left and the landscape is in the centre.
- The still life is not next to the photograph.
- Bill's seascape hangs next to Farid's artwork, which is not the landscape.
- Vic's work is somewhere to the right of Dane's and to the left of Abe's.
- The photograph is not next to Dane's artwork.

Whose work is the still life?

A Abe   B Dane

C Farid   D Vic

28 Auslan is the sign language of the Australian Deaf community. Learning Auslan as a second language enables people with hearing impairment to communicate with each other as well as with people who are not hearing impaired. Auslan is not just English through signing, it is a distinct visual language with its own structures and features. Auslan should be taught in all schools. The more Auslan users there are, the more inclusive our society will be.

Which one of these statements, if true, most **weakens** the above argument?

A Auslan is not taught in some schools due to lack of trained teachers.

B One in six Australians are affected by hearing loss.

C Thirty thousand deaf people use Auslan in Australia.

D Learning Auslan improves memory and stimulates the brain.

☞ **Answers and explanations on pages 56–62**

29 David, Isabel and Julia are playing a game. They each begin with 20 counters. They take it in turns to roll a dice. If an even number is rolled, the player receives that number of counters from each of the other players. If an odd number is rolled, the player must give that number of counters to each of the others.

After the first round of three rolls, David has 9 counters. In that round David rolled a 3 and Isabel rolled a 1. How many counters will Julia have after the first round?

A 15   B 24   C 30   D 36

30 Many gardeners complain about caterpillars eating the plants in their garden but without those caterpillars we would not have butterflies. Butterflies play a vital role in the environment. Like bees, butterflies pollinate plants. They are also an important part of the food cycle. Butterflies, and their caterpillars or chrysalises, provide a food source for birds, lizards, small mammals and spiders. If butterfly populations shrink, the impact is felt higher up the food chain. It can affect the entire ecosystem. Sadly butterflies have been deeply impacted by a warming climate, habitat loss and the use of pesticides but you can help by not reaching for the pesticide — and allowing butterflies to lay caterpillar eggs in your garden.

Which one of these statements, if true, most **strengthens** the above argument?

A There are over 230 000 species of butterflies and moths around the world.

B Each species of butterfly is beautiful and unique.

C In the past decade there has been a 50% decline in butterfly populations around the world.

D Scientists use the presence or absence of butterflies as a predictor of whether an ecosystem is healthy.

31 While Zoe, Ray, Tarek and Bev were playing, a vase was broken. Their mother asked: 'Who broke the vase?' Their replies were:
Zoe: 'It wasn't me.'
Ray: 'You're lying Zoe; it was you.'
Tarek: 'It wasn't Zoe; it was Ray.'
Bev: 'It wasn't me.'

The only person who lied was the one who broke the vase. Who was it?

A Zoe   B Ray   C Tarek   D Bev

32

To be a successful wildlife ranger, you need to be incredibly strong: mentally, physically and emotionally. You need to be able to make accurate observations and recordings. You need to be able to walk rugged terrain and long distances. And you need to be able to handle animals with confidence and patience. You must also be interested in conservation and science.

Summer: 'Mia won the cross-country race last term and in the holidays she rescued an injured possum. She's on the sustainability committee at school and she came first in science. She'd be a successful wildlife ranger for sure.'

Jack: 'Alex is really fit. He goes rock climbing and runs in marathons. He also volunteers at the local bush regeneration project. But I don't think he likes science. So wildlife ranger is definitely not for him.'

If the information in the box is true, whose reasoning is correct?

A Summer only

B Jack only

C Both Summer and Jack

D Neither Summer nor Jack

33 The numbers from 1 to 9 have been replaced with letters so that all the sums, both across and down, are correct. Every number is replaced by a different letter.

PP	+	NL	=	KNE
+		+		+
FE	+	FL	=	GN
=		=		=
KFK	+	PH	=	ELQ

Which is **not** correct?

A N = 5

B Q = 6

C G = 8

D P = 9

34 A train left Brighton for London at 3 pm and a second train left London for Brighton at the same time. The first train was half as fast as the second train and arrived at London at 6 pm. The trains travelled at a constant speed and made no stops.

At what time did the trains pass each other?

A 3:45 pm

B 4 pm

C 4:30 pm

D 5 pm

35 Mr Pig is at the police station to file a report. He says that while he was at the market yesterday, someone blew down his house made of sticks. He suspects that the wrongdoer was Mr Wolf. The police officer tells Mr Pig that whoever blew down the house must be very strong and must have been in the area yesterday.

Based on the above information, which conclusion must be true?

A If Mr Wolf did not blow down the house, he must not have been in the area yesterday.

B If Mr Wolf had a cold and was very weak, he cannot have blown down the house.

C If Mr Wolf did not blow down the house, he cannot be very strong.

D If Mr Wolf is very strong and also was in the area yesterday, he must have blown down the house.

36 Ernie wants to tile the floor in his laundry. He will use some triangular tiles, all with the same pattern. Which of the following patterns is it **impossible** for him to create?

A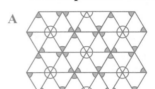

B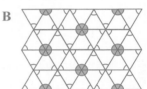

C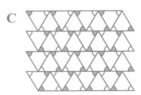

D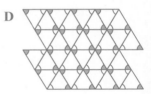

37 Graham and a friend use their own personal code, which is made using their own name, when writing messages to each other.

Here is the code that Graham uses:

A	B	C	D	E	F	G	H	I	J	K	L	M
G	R	A	H	M	B	C	D	E	F	I	J	K
N	**O**	**P**	**Q**	**R**	**S**	**T**	**U**	**V**	**W**	**X**	**Y**	**Z**
L	N	O	P	Q	S	T	U	V	W	X	Y	Z

Graham and his friend each use their own code to write the same word.

Graham writes RQMGH.

His friend writes EQAPY.

What could his friend's name be?

A Peter

B Eadie

C Penny

D Zenya

38 There are two ways to qualify to enter the annual State Junior Film Contest: by entering at least three other smaller film contests during the year or by winning any other film contest during the year.

This year six students from Sanjay's school have qualified to enter the State Junior Film Contest.

Sanjay: 'I know a total of four films by students at our school have won contests during the year. So that means more than half our qualifiers must be contest winners.'

Which one of the following sentences shows the mistake Sanjay has made?

A Some students may have won more than one film contest during the year.

B Some students may have entered more than three film contests during the year.

C The number of films made during the year may be higher than in other years.

D Some students who won film contests in the past may also have entered three other film contests during the year.

39 The manager of a timber company said in a television interview: 'Growing trees on large-scale plantations is good for the environment. Our timber is renewable, recyclable and energy efficient to produce on our single-species plantations. As it grows, our planation timber acts as a carbon store and so plays an important role in reducing carbon emissions.'

Which one of these statements, if true, most **weakens** the manager's claim?

A Large-scale tree plantations often replace native forests.

B Old-growth, diverse forests store carbon for centuries.

C Experts predict a massive increase in single-species tree plantations.

D Studies show that single-species tree plantations emit more carbon than they absorb.

40 If several dice are rolled and show consecutive values, they are said to be 'in sequence'. The 'total of all dice' is the sum of the values showing on the top of the dice. For example, the three dice below are in sequence and the total of all dice is 6.

Freya rolls five normal dice and four of them are in sequence. The total of all five dice is 19.

Which statement is **not** true?

A If Freya rolled a 2, she also rolled a 1.

B If Freya rolled a 2, she also rolled two 5s.

C If Freya rolled a 6, she also rolled a 1.

D If Freya rolled a 6, she didn't roll a 2.

SAMPLE TEST 2

1 This pattern is part of a tiled wall. It is made up of six identical square tiles, although some have been rotated. A section of the tiles has been covered by a power point.

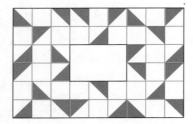

What would the covered part look like?

A   **B**

C   **D**

2 To have a chance of winning the scholarship you must have proven both your ability as well as your commitment.

Sally: 'I did not win the scholarship.'

If the information in the box is true, which statement shows incorrect reasoning?

A If Sally did not win the scholarship, she cannot have proven her commitment.

B If Sally did not win the scholarship, she cannot have proven her ability.

C If Sally did not prove her commitment as well as her ability, she could not have won the scholarship.

D If Sally proved her ability and her commitment, she must have won the scholarship.

3 There are five beds in a row in a dormitory. Each bed is covered with a different coloured blanket. Five boys, George, Hiro, Isaac, Oliver and Zac, each sleep in one of the beds at a school camp. The boys are all different ages from 8 to 12.

- Isaac sleeps in the bed with the yellow blanket on the far right.
- The oldest boy has the bed with the brown blanket.
- The bed with the blue blanket is next to Hiro's bed.
- Zac, who is 9, sleeps in the bed next to Oliver, who is 10.
- George's bed with the green blanket is directly between the bed with the red blanket and the bed where the 11-year-old sleeps.

What colour is the blanket on the bed that is in the centre of the row?

A blue   **B** brown **C** green   **D** red

4 Patrick needs to travel from Clifford to Smithton by train, and home again, every day beginning on Wednesday and finishing on the following Tuesday. He knows that it costs $4 for a one-way trip and $6 for a return (two-way) ticket. A weekly ticket costs $17 for travel from Monday to Friday of any one week. A weekend pass costs $5 for any travel anywhere over the weekend.

What is the lowest price that Patrick can pay for his travel?

A $28   **B** $34   **C** $35   **D** $39

5 When completed all three rows, all three columns and both diagonals of this magic square add to the same total.

8		
6		5

What is that total?

A 30   **B** 27   **C** 24   **D** 21

☞ **Answers and explanations on pages 62–67**

6 To be awarded one of the school's 'Sports Participation' prizes for the month you need to have participated in four sporting activities yourself over the month or to have been a volunteer assistant coach on eight occasions for sporting activities with a younger age group. At the end of July, twenty students received a 'Sports Participation' prize.

Naseem: 'I know that in July eight students coached younger groups at least nine times a week, five students coached younger groups on eight occasions and one student coached younger students in soccer eight times. So that means six students won a 'Sports Participation' prize for participating in four sporting activities over the month.'

Which one of the following sentences shows the mistake Naseem has made?

A Naseem thinks everyone who got a 'Sports Participation' prize for volunteer assistant coaching also received one for participating in four sporting activities.

B Naseem does not know how many students missed out on a 'Sports Participation' prize.

C Naseem doesn't realise that some of the prizewinners may have been a volunteer assistant coach on a minimum of eight occasions and also participated in four sporting activities themselves.

D Naseem thinks some students have received a prize they did not deserve.

7 A piece of a three-dimensional puzzle is shown below.

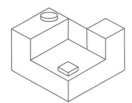

Which piece below will fit with the piece above to make a cube?

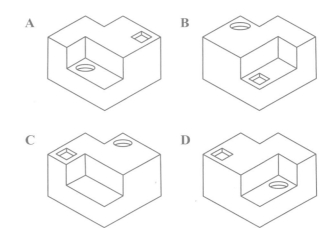

8 The Great Barrier Reef is the largest living organism on earth but it is under threat from the impacts of climate change. Ocean temperatures are rising, causing coral bleaching and impacting the health of the reef ecosystem. Oceans are absorbing more carbon dioxide from the atmosphere and this leads to acidification of the ocean, which impacts the coral. More severe and more frequent extreme weather events, such as hurricanes, damage the reef. Scientists worry that time is running out on action for climate change to save the Great Barrier Reef. Without urgent action to prevent further climate change, the Great Barrier Reef will die.

If the information in the box is correct, which statement below most **strengthens** the argument?

A Urgent global action to reduce greenhouse gas emissions is essential to have any hope of saving the reef.

B Coral reefs support 25% of all marine life so protecting reefs protects people.

C Pesticides and agricultural run-off into the ocean affects the water quality on the reef.

D Ocean acidification causes the coral to eject its polyps and therefore turn completely white.

9 To receive one of the Achievement Awards for athletics at the school carnival, competitors need to have competed in at least four events and finished first, second or third in three of them.

If the above information is correct, which one of the following sentences **cannot** be true?

A Competitors can win an Achievement Award even if they come third in three out of three events.

B If you finish first, second or third in three events, you can come last in the fourth event and still get an Achievement Award.

C An overall champion will be a good competitor but not necessarily the best athlete at the school.

D Some competitors could compete in more than four events but not receive an Achievement Award.

10 In the following diagram, the large cogs have 12 teeth each, the medium cog has eight teeth and the small cog has six teeth. The two cogs in the middle are connected by a belt (like a bike chain) that means they make one full revolution in the same amount of time.

The cog on the left is turned one full rotation. How many rotations will the cog on the right make?

A one

B one and one-third

C one and two-thirds

D two

11 The oldest mine in the world is the Ngwenya Mine in Eswatini. Ancestors of the San People mined there 40 000 years ago. They mined the red ochres used in rituals, rock paintings and cosmetics. In 400 AD the Bantu people moved into the area and Ngwenya Mine became an iron-ore mine. The Bantu knew how to smelt iron ore and they traded iron. Open-pit mining took place between 1964 and 1977. Ngwenya means crocodile in Swazi. The mountains were crocodile shaped before open-pit mining took place. In recent decades the mine has been linked to corruption scandals and environmental and cultural vandalism.

Which statement can be concluded from the above information?

A Stone-age artifacts have been found on the site, proving the mine's age and cultural significance.

B In recent decades the mine has been linked to corruption scandals and environmental and cultural vandalism.

C Open-pit mining radically changes landscapes.

D The Bantu People were less advanced technologically than the San People.

12 Katy is excited because her school is holding a Short Film Festival. Each student is allowed to enter only one short film they have made into the festival contest. Judges will score the films and trophies will be awarded for first, second and third place. Plus there is also a trophy for People's Choice which will be voted for by the audience on the night of the festival.

Katy: 'That means four entrants will get trophies!'

Which one of the following sentences shows the mistake Katy has made?

A One student might be awarded a trophy for more than one film.

B Some films might be disqualified.

C We don't know how many films will be entered in the contest.

D The People's Choice trophy winner might also come first, second or third.

13 At a movie marathon, ticket holders can choose to see four movies in a row from the timetable below. They must only choose one film from each session.

Session 1	Session 2	Session 3	Session 4
Red Dog	Ratatouille	Clifford	Bambi
Cats	Red Dog	Milo and Otis	Beethoven
Beethoven	Milo and Otis	Red Dog 2	Clifford
Milo and Otis	Red Dog 2	101 Dalmatians	Ratatouille

Charissa wants to see *Red Dog* at some point before *Red Dog 2*, as well as *101 Dalmatians*. Which movie can she definitely **not** see?

A *Milo and Otis*

B *Ratatouille*

C *Clifford*

D *Bambi*

14 Five friends entered an obstacle race. They had to run a 5-kilometre course with 20 obstacles.

- Levi was slower than Rose but Rose was slower than Grace.
- George cleared all the obstacles but took the longest.
- Rose finished second but missed two obstacles.
- Ethan cleared more obstacles than Rose but finished after her.
- Grace was faster than Ethan but missed three obstacles.

If the above information is true, which one of the sentences below **cannot** be true?

A Ethan cleared fewer obstacles than George.

B Grace was faster than Levi.

C Grace was not the first to finish the course.

D Grace cleared the least number of obstacles.

15 When Anita told Wei she was going to quit the weekend bushwalking club because she wanted to do well in the final exams so had to spend every weekend studying, Wei said: 'You don't have to quit bushwalking just because you need to study. You could work really hard and then take a break to come on the walk. The break would do you good and help you study!'

Which one of these statements, if true, most **strengthens** Wei's argument?

A Research shows that spending time outdoors leads to better focus.

B A new study found that outdoor activities improve leadership skills.

C It's hard to make outdoor time a priority when we are busy.

D Anita is already top of the class.

16 Kirby visits the debating club every Monday, Wednesday and Thursday. A particular month begins on a Tuesday and in that month she visits the club exactly 14 times. How many days are in that month?

A 28   B 29   C 30   D 31

17 A cafe owner surveyed customers to find out what they would like added to the menu. The cafe found that anyone who was in favour of nachos was also in favour of fresh juices. Anyone in favour of fresh juices was in favour of a salad bar but no-one who was in favour of fresh juices was in favour of protein balls.

Based on the above information, which conclusion **must** be true?

A If Taj is not in favour of protein balls, he does not want a salad bar.

B If Norbit is in favour of nachos, he does not want protein balls.

C If Zoe is not in favour of nachos, she does not want a salad bar.

D If Clara is in favour of a salad bar, she is also in favour of fresh juices.

18 Mr Lee teaches piano. At the end of each term he gives each of his students an exam. Each student is given a score for performance of a piece and a score for technical skills, such as scales. The performance score and the technical score are then added together to give a final exam score.

Nia and Blake just found out that they got the same final exam score.

Nia: 'If we each got a different score for performance, then our scores for technical skills must have been different too.'

Blake: 'If our performance scores were the same, then our scores for technical skills must have been the same too.'

Based on the information in the box, whose reasoning is correct?

A Nia

B Blake

C Both Nia and Blake

D Neither Nia nor Blake

19 A group of people were asked which of five types of music they enjoy. Once the results were tallied, the following statements were made.

- All of those who like country like classical.
- Some of those who like pop like country.
- Some of those who like rap like pop.
- None of those who like both pop and rap like classical.
- Some of those who like jazz like country.

One man who likes jazz likes three types of music only. Which two other types can he **not** also like?

A rap and classical

B pop and rap

C country and pop

D classical and country

20 To win a poetry recitation award you need to show confidence. Choose a poem you love and understand. Use your voice and project it clearly. Pronounce every word correctly, use appropriate dramatic presentation and make eye contact with your audience.

This year there are five categories of award to win plus the overall winner award.

Jayden: 'I know Scarlet rushes her recitation when she's nervous. If she shows she's nervous, she won't win a prize but if she can overcome her nerves and not rush her presentation, she has a good chance of winning a prize.'

Conor: 'I know Eden tends to overact when she recites because she loves being on stage and performing live theatre. If she can tone down the acting and use appropriate dramatic presentation, I think she could win a prize.'

If the information in the box is true, whose reasoning is correct?

A Jayden only

B Conor only

C Both Jayden and Conor

D Neither Jayden nor Conor

21 Carmel counted the number of legs on all the stools in a fast-food restaurant. Some of the stools had four legs and the rest had just three. She counted 61 legs altogether. If there were 18 stools in the restaurant, how many had four legs?

A 7   B 8   C 10   D 11

22 Housing growth is the main cause of habitat loss world-wide. Habitat loss is a direct result of urban sprawl (housing and associated roads, shopping facilities and other infrastructure spreading further out from cities and towns). Housing growth also increases pollution and other risks to the natural environment and brings with it the threat of domestic predators to native animals.

If the above information is true, which conclusion **cannot** be true?

A Containing urban sprawl will limit the need for housing.

B Habitat loss means more land available for housing.

C To protect native animals we need to protect their habitats.

D Effective land management involves planning for a balance of urban development and habitat protection.

23 Five people stood for election as a council representative. The table shows the results.

Name	Number of votes
Aziz	36
Greg	18
Patricia	30
Theo	24
Una	12

A graph was then drawn but unfortunately the graph was not labelled and Una's votes were added to those for someone else.

Who received Una's votes on the graph?

A Aziz   B Greg   C Patricia   D Theo

24 Sanjeer says: 'Rules for using an electric scooter vary from state to state in Australia. In some parts of Australia people are allowed to ride electric scooters on public footpaths. The scooters don't have to be registered and people don't need a licence to ride them but riders need to wear helmets, are not allowed to carry passengers and must comply with speed limits. Due to perceived dangers, other parts of Australia ban or limit electric-scooter use except on private property. I think there should be one set of rules for scooter use across the whole of Australia.'

Which one of these statements, if true, most **strengthens** Sanjeer's argument?

A The National Transport Commission recommended capping the e-scooter speed limit on cycle paths to 25 km/h and on footpaths to 10 km/h.

B If you travel from state to state in Australia, you never know what the rules for scooter use are and you could be fined.

C One study of e-scooter accidents found that riding an e-scooter is 100 times more dangerous than riding a bicycle.

D Some people ride e-scooters too fast on footpaths where pedestrians can get hurt.

25 Five people, Abid, Joseph, Leo, Molly and Stella, competed in a trivia competition. They all achieved different scores.

■ Abid took the longest but got all 10 questions correct.

■ Molly was faster than Stella but got two questions wrong.

■ Joseph got fewer questions right than Stella but finished after her.

■ Leo got more questions wrong than Joseph but finished before Molly.

Which one of the following statements **cannot** be true?

A Leo finished first.

B Molly finished third.

C Stella got only one question wrong.

D Joseph got at least three questions wrong.

26 Lots of people in Australia love reading about and watching news items about the British royal family.

Natalie says: 'Sadly many people don't think beyond the fairytale lives of princes and princesses. They don't consider that members of royal families don't earn their right to have status, wealth and power. They inherited these privileges and their money and power are the result of colonialism.'

Which one of these statements, if true, most **weakens** Natalie's argument?

A To celebrate and admire the British monarchy you have to ignore its role in colonisation.

B Many Australians have arrived in Australia from places with a colonial past.

C Monarchies unite people in feeling national pride.

D Australia's First Nations Peoples have no reason to celebrate the British royal family.

27 Dave, Rachel, Sonia, Terry and Wes each live in a different villa on a certain street. They all have a different number of children, from 0 to 4. The villas are numbered 1 to 5 from left to right.

	1	2	3	4	5	
left						right

The person with two children lives three villas to the right of Sonia.

The person with one child lives two villas to the right of Terry.

Dave's villa number is even but the villa where the person with three children lives is odd.

Wes lives the same number of places right of the villa where there are no children as he lives left of the villa with four children.

How many children does Sonia have?

A 0   B 1   C 3   D 4

28 'Whoever picked the parsley from the communal herb garden must have had both a motive and an opportunity.'

If this is true, which one of these statements must also be true?

A If Amelia did not have an opportunity to pick the parsley, she must have been the one to take it.

B If Amelia picked the parsley, she cannot have had a motive.

C If Amelia picked the parsley, she cannot have had an opportunity.

D If Amelia did not have a motive, she cannot have picked the parsley.

29 Four boys are talking about a black-and-white bird they had seen. They make these statements:

Alexander: 'It was a magpie.'
Frank: 'It wasn't a peewee.'
George: 'It wasn't a magpie.'
Steven: 'It was a currawong.'

Three of the boys were correct, but one got it wrong.

Which boy got it wrong?

A Alexander
B Frank
C George
D Steven

30 A doctor claimed that a particular vaccination always worked to prevent a certain disease. An experiment with two patients was carried out.

Patient	Has been vaccinated	Caught the disease
Lisa	P	Yes
Max	Yes	Q

Which is the only result that doesn't prove the doctor wrong?

A P is Yes and Q is Yes.
B P is Yes and Q is No.
C P is No and Q is Yes.
D P is No and Q is No.

31 Max's school was selecting students to attend a special music camp. As well as considering their regular attendance at band rehearsals, the music teacher set them a test and a teamwork challenge.

If a student had regularly attended band rehearsals, then they only had to pass the music test in order to be selected to attend. If a student had not regularly attended band rehearsals, then they either needed to get an excellent result in the music test, or do well in both the music test and the teamwork challenge.

Max had regularly attended band rehearsals but failed to be selected to attend the music camp. What must have been the reason?

A Max failed the music test.

B Max did badly in the teamwork challenge.

C Max had not regularly attended band rehearsals.

D Max did well in the music test but badly in the teamwork challenge.

32 Ella wrote a letter to the local newspaper. She suggested that, instead of grass, people should plant native gardens on their nature strips. She said that nature strips could then be oases of biodiversity rather than nightmares of patchy grass that take a long time to mow and still look barren.

Which one of these statements, if true, most **strengthens** Ella's argument?

A Nature strip gardens should not block the vision of passing traffic.

B Native gardens have more biodiversity than grass lawns.

C Some people have planted community vegetable gardens in their backyards.

D Once a native nature strip is established, maintenance is virtually nil.

33 Latika owns a very old pocket watch that runs slightly slowly. It only moves 50 minutes for every hour. Latika synchronised her watch to the clock at the Town Hall at 10:30 am before going on a walk.

When she checked her watch a little later, it showed 11:30 am. For how long had she been walking?

A 50 minutes

B 1 hour

C 1 hour 6 minutes

D 1 hour 12 minutes

34 EasyBus hires out buses at the following rates.

	Price per day for duration of hire			
	1 day	2–3 days	4–5 days	6+ days
8-seater	$1000	$800	$700	$650
12-seater	$1200	$1000	$900	$850
28-seater	$1500	$1300	$1200	$1150

15 friends going on a footy trip want to hire a bus for 4 days, splitting the cost evenly between them. How much will each person pay?

A $80

B $100

C $320

D $400

35

> Most penguins waddle. But Eastern Rockhopper penguins are able to jump from one rock to another. They are also the only known penguin species to jump feet first into the water when they dive.

Zeynep: 'If you see a penguin jump feet first into the water, you know it must be an Eastern Rockhopper.'

Hugo: 'And if you see a penguin waddling, then it can't be an Eastern Rockhopper.'

If the information in the box is true, whose reasoning is correct?

A Zeynep only

B Hugo only

C Both Zeynep and Hugo

D Neither Zeynep nor Hugo

36 Tessa wants to use a single square tile design to cover the floor of her bathroom. Each of the following patterns is made using 16 tiles. Which of the following patterns is the only one she can possibly use?

A 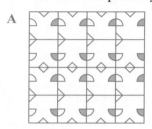   B

C 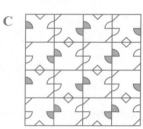   D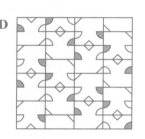

37 A piece of a three-dimensional puzzle is shown below.

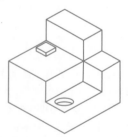

Which piece below will fit with the piece above to make a cube?

A 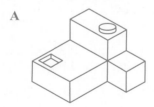   B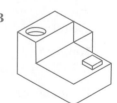

C 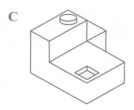   D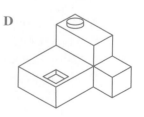

38 Aisha has a test tomorrow.

If she stays up late tonight, then she'll likely be tired tomorrow.

If she is tired, then she will not do well in the test.

If she does well in the test, then she might be offered a scholarship. Otherwise she doesn't stand a chance.

If the above statements are correct, which one of the following is **not** possible?

A Aisha stayed up late but got the scholarship.

B Aisha did well in the test but did not get the scholarship.

C Aisha was tired but did well in the test and got the scholarship.

D Aisha went to bed early but did not get the scholarship.

39

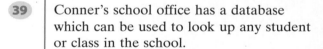

Conner's school office has a database which can be used to look up any student or class in the school.

Conner: 'If you know the first name of a student, you don't need to know which class they are in—you can look it up in the database.'

Which one of the following sentences shows the mistake Conner has made?

A Some classes have new students.

B Some classes have more students than other classes.

C Some students have the same first name as each other.

D There are some students who are absent.

SAMPLE TEST 2

40 In the diagram below, there are two different paths around the square that can be taken to reach B from A.

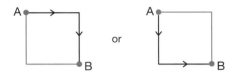

How many different paths can be taken to reach B from A in the following diagram? You must always move in such a way that the distance to B is getting smaller. That is, you must only move down or to the right. You cannot move up or to the left.

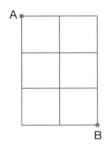

A 6
B 8
C 10
D 12

40 MIN

1 Ben, Jake, Lewis, Abdul and Timothy played in the same soccer team. In the last game, Abdul scored 7 more goals than Lewis. Ben and Jake scored the same number of goals. Lewis scored 2 fewer goals than Jake. Timothy scored more goals than Jake, but fewer than Abdul. Ben scored 10 goals.

Only one of the following sentences must be true. Which is it?

A Timothy scored 12 goals.

B Abdul scored 15 goals.

C Abdul scored 4 more goals than Jake.

D All the boys scored more than 9 goals.

2 When Julia told Lei she was giving up her part-time job as a DJ to focus on becoming a full-time musician, Lei said: 'You don't need to give up being a DJ to become a full-time musician. You enjoy being a DJ and you earn some money at the same time. There's no need to stop being a DJ on Friday nights.'

Which one of these statements, if true, most **strengthens** Lei's argument?

A Any work in the music and entertainment industry supports a career as a musician.

B Julia is struggling to find enough work as a musician.

C Lei is a very popular DJ.

D Being a DJ is a highly skilled job that requires continual practice in order to improve.

3 Ehab, Lachlan, Stathis, Thomas and Xavier filled the top five places in a race. They each wore a different-coloured shirt: blue, green, red, white or yellow.

Lachlan came first and the boy in blue came third.

Stathis finished somewhere after the boy in yellow and somewhere before Thomas.

Xavier finished after, but not immediately after, Ehab and before the boy in red.

The boy in the green shirt finished just before Stathis.

What colour shirt did Xavier wear?

A blue

B green

C white

D yellow

4 Derek, Hung and Matt play a game. They begin with 25 marbles each and take turns to roll a dice.

If they roll an even number, they receive two marbles from each of the others, but if they roll an odd number, they must give one marble to each of the others.

After they have all rolled the dice once, Derek has 31 marbles. How many marbles will Hung have?

A 20   B 21   C 22   D 23

5 Camels are not native to Australia. They were brought to Australia in the 1840s and used to transport goods across the outback. It is estimated there are hundreds of thousands of feral camels in Australia. They destroy fencing, foul water sources, and eat native vegetation such as curly pod wattle, bean tree, quandong, plumbush and supplejack, thereby depriving native animals of food. Camels also disturb important First Australian sites and contribute to erosion by destabilising sand dunes. Feral camel populations are difficult to manage.

If this is true, which one of these sentences must also be true?

A Feral camels roam over wide distances so strong fencing is needed to protect sensitive environmental areas.

B Camels are well adapted to survival in very dry areas across Australia.

C Aerial shooting seems to be the most humane way to cull camels in remote areas.

D Camels were useful to people transporting goods across the outback.

6 A tourist attraction has tickets at $10 for 1 day or special prices for combinations of different numbers of days, all taken consecutively (in a row). Those special prices are $18 for 2 days, $32 for 4 days and $50 for 7 days. Samuel wants to visit the attraction on these 10 dates in January: 3, 4, 5, 19, 20, 21, 25, 26, 27 and 28.

What is the least amount he could pay for his tickets?

A $78   **B** $82   **C** $88   **D** $96

7 Sea dragons and seahorses are close relatives. They are bony fishes. Seahorses live in tropical and subtropical waters all over the world. Sea dragons only live in Australian waters. The two creatures have similar body and head shapes but sea dragons have longer snouts and longer tails. The sea dragon's tail does not curl like a sea horse's tail, which is used to hold onto plants and other things as anchors.

Seahorses have stiff spines while sea dragons have leafy appendages that look like seaweed. Male seahorses have a stomach pouch for their eggs. Male sea dragons carry their eggs on a patch on the underside of their tails.

Ava: 'If you see a fish with a horse's head and a long tail in the waters around Australia, you know it must be a seahorse.'

Fawad: 'If you see a fish with a horse's head, a long snout and a long tail you know it must be a sea dragon.'

If the information in the box is true, whose reasoning is correct?

A Ava only

B Fawad only

C Both Ava and Fawad

D Neither Ava nor Fawad

8 This puzzle is made up of 15 squares all divided into triangles. The triangles in each square are numbered from 1 to 4. Wherever the squares adjoin, the two numbers must be the same. For example, the top number in the first square on the middle row must be 4 and the bottom number of that square must be 1.

When the puzzle is complete, what number must go into the shaded triangle?

A 1   **B** 2   **C** 3   **D** 4

9 Hamish is a member of the debating team. Debaters have been warned that any debater will be dismissed if they miss three practices in a month without a good excuse or for any incidence of inadequate written preparation for a debate. Inadequate preparation is severely frowned upon because it is disrespectful to other debaters who have taken the time to prepare and can cause the team to lose. Positions on the debating team are highly prized and Hamish knows that if he does not perform well or if he slips up in any way, he can lose his place on the team.

If the above statements are correct, which one of the following is **not** possible?

A Hamish prepared inadequately but was not dismissed from the team.

B Hamish missed three practices in a month without a good excuse and was dismissed.

C Hamish attended all the practices and did adequate preparation but was dismissed.

D Hamish had a good excuse for not showing up for rehearsals so was not dismissed.

10 A piece of a puzzle is shown below.

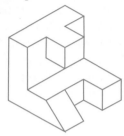

Which one of the following pieces could fit with the piece above to make a cube?

A

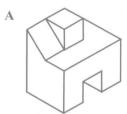

B

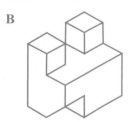

C

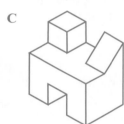

D

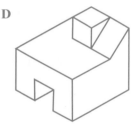

11 In the Junior Scrabble Tournament, cash prizes are given to the players who come first, second or third and to the player who makes the highest scoring move of the day.

Sienna: 'There are four cash prizes to be won at the tournament so four children will go home with prize money. I hope I am one of them.'

Which one of the following sentences shows the mistake Sienna has made?

A Some players might not be able to accept a cash prize.

B We are not told the number of players competing at the tournament.

C The highest scoring play might have been made by a player who came first, second or third.

D Some players might earn a prize for participation.

12 To become a therapy dog, a dog needs to get along well with people, including young children and the elderly. It must be able to handle sudden loud or strange noises and also be able to walk comfortably on different unfamiliar surfaces and in unfamiliar situations.

Luca: 'Muffin comes everywhere with us. She doesn't care where we go, as long as she gets to come along. We even took her to see the fireworks and she wasn't bothered by all the noise and people. She'd be a great therapy dog for sure.'

Uma: 'Scamp loves people. He loves playing with my little brother. And he's so gentle when he greets my grandma and is careful not to knock her walking stick. But he sometimes hides under the bed when there's thunder so he might have a problem with loud noises. Being a therapy dog is probably not for him.'

If the information in the box is true, whose reasoning is correct?

A Luca only

B Uma only

C Both Luca and Uma

D Neither Luca nor Uma

13 In a system of rope and pulleys, the number of pulleys corresponds to how much force is needed to lift a weight.

The force required to lift a weight using a system of two pulleys is half that of the force required to lift it without one.

The force required to lift a weight using a system of three pulleys is one-third that of the force required to lift it without one.

This pattern continues.

Hafthor can apply enough force to a rope to lift a maximum of 116 kg with a system of four pulleys. What is the maximum he can lift with a system of seven pulleys?

A 187 kg

B 203 kg

C 232 kg

D 928 kg

14 It's quite common for doctors to talk about how unhealthy it is to sit for too long and why people should therefore stand up more. But a physiotherapist argues that standing up more is just the start. He says the problem is that we tend to stick to limited positions when we sleep, walk, sit and stand. He recommends changing position every 30 minutes and moving around as much as possible—because any position held for too long is bad news, even a good position.

Which one of these statements, if true, most **strengthens** the physiotherapist's argument?

A It is better to use a cross-body bag than a shoulder bag to better balance your body.

B Ballet dancers perform the same repetitive positions and suffer pain and health issues despite their perfect posture.

C Moving more, and in a variety of positions, is the key to better health.

D We tend to sleep, walk, sit and stand the same ways every day.

15 The drama club teacher said that any students who did not get a chance to perform in the play last term will definitely be given the chance to perform this term.

Kala: 'Oh no, I was in the play last term. That means I won't be allowed to perform this term. I'll have to find another club to join!'

Which one of the following sentences shows the mistake Kala has made?

A Just because someone did not get a chance to perform last term, it does not mean that they would not have liked to perform.

B Just because Kala was in the play last term, it does not mean that she will be selected to be in it this term.

C Just because anyone who did not get a chance to be in the play last term will be given a chance to be in it this term, it does not mean that anyone who was in it last term will not be able to be in it again this term.

D Just because someone did not get a chance to be in the play last term, it does not mean that they will be given a chance to be in it this term.

16 Pete and Kima aim to meet for lunch at 1 pm. Pete leaves his home at 12:10 pm and walks to the restaurant, arriving at 12:52 pm. Kima leaves her home at 12:30 pm and arrives at the restaurant at 1:03 pm. If they both leave lunch at exactly the same time, who will arrive home first and by how many minutes? (They both take the same time to walk home as they took to walk to the restaurant.)

A Kima by 9 minutes

B Pete by 9 minutes

C Kima by 11 minutes

D Pete by 11 minutes

17 The local council announced it would hold traditional fireworks on New Year's Eve.

The mayor said: 'Drones and laser lightshows are a higher cost compared to fireworks. They also take more time to design and the regulations and permits required are more complex. For these reasons Council found these eco-friendly substitutes to be of little value to our ratepayers.'

Which one of these statements, if true, most **weakens** the mayor's claim?

A 90% of ratepayers are in favour of eco-friendly substitutes for fireworks.

B A Council committee reviewed alternatives to fireworks.

C Laser lightshows have a higher risk of poor display due to weather.

D Traditional firework displays will be held in multiple locations across the local area.

18 A sports reporter said: 'Whoever won the athletic championship must have had both the athletic skill and the ability to perform in competition conditions.'

If this is true, which one of these sentences must also be true?

A If Atiya did not win the athletic championship, she must not have had the ability to perform in competition conditions.

B If Breno has athletic skill and the ability to perform in competition conditions, he must have won the athletic championship.

C If Stella did not win the athletic championship, she must not have athletic skill.

D If Kale did not have the ability to perform in competition conditions, he cannot have won the athletic championship.

19 Nathan is working on this puzzle. He has four more pieces to put in, in the spaces labelled *P*, *Q*, *R* and *S*.

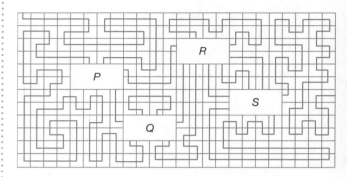

Which piece will fit in the puzzle in the space marked *P*?

A 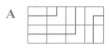   B

C    D

20 Three people, Sarah, Nicole and Kate, are accused of stealing a gold watch. Under interrogation, each makes a statement.

Sarah says: 'I didn't steal it.'

Nicole says: 'I didn't steal it.'

Kate says: 'Sarah stole it.'

It turns out that only one of the three is lying.

What **cannot** be true?

A Sarah stole the watch.

B Nicole stole the watch.

C Kate stole the watch.

D Someone else stole the watch.

21 Electrical appliances in Australia have a star rating that shows their energy efficiency. Buying appliances with four- and five-star ratings can help people save on their power bills. Every extra star on an appliance's rating is equal to a 20% reduction in its electricity consumption. In recent years Australian standards have fallen behind Europe and the United States. Some products for sale in Australia are so energy inefficient they would not be allowed on sale in Europe or the United States. Australia could do a lot better with its energy efficiency if it had higher standards.

Based on the above information, which one of the following **cannot** be true?

A The Australia energy star rating on appliances is not working as well as it should.

B Europe and the United States have higher standards than Australia for energy-efficient appliances.

C A one-star rating is more energy efficient than a five-star rating.

D Introducing higher standards would benefit consumers.

22 At the end of each week Mr Seneweera gives scores in reading, writing and oral language to give each student an overall score for English for the week. For example, a student with a score of 15 in reading, 15 in writing and 10 in oral language will have an overall English score of 40.

Last week Mehreen and Mitchell tied in English.

Mehreen: 'If our scores were the same in reading and writing, then our oral language score must have been the same too.'

Mitchell: 'If my reading score was the same as your writing score and our oral language scores were the same as each other, then my writing score must have been the same as your reading score.'

If the information in the box is true, whose reasoning is correct?

A Mehreen only

B Mitchell only

C Both Mehreen and Mitchell

D Neither Mehreen nor Mitchell

23 Donations needed!

Our school is fundraising to support an Active Inclusion Sports Day to be delivered by Disability Sports Australia at Netball Central. The aim of the day is to support people with disabilities to be more active for better health outcomes.

This is a free event for students aged from 5 to 18 who have physical, intellectual or sensory disabilities and/ or learning difficulties. Students will be able to try a number of modified sporting activities and appropriate equipment.

Please give generously!
Alya

Which one of these statements, if true, most **strengthens** Alya's argument?

A Local Councils, State Sporting Organisations, Universities, NDIS and State Government Departments have collaborated to provide Active Inclusion Sports Day.

B Increased activity promotes physical health as well as mental health.

C Mental health is supported through building friendships and community engagement.

D Students can develop independence and self-esteem in an inclusive environment.

24 A piece of A4 paper was folded in half, then folded in half again, then folded in half again. A triangle was cut from the piece of paper and the paper was unfolded.

Which is the only possible view of the unfolded piece of paper?

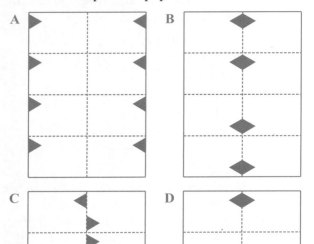

A

B

C

D

25 AdventureTime runs fishing trips for small groups of people with prices shown in the following chart.

No. people	Duration of trip			
	3 hours	6 hours	9 hours	12 hours
1–2	$360	$540	$700	$970
3–6	$510	$765	$995	$1380
7–10	$945	$1420	$1850	$2550

Five friends decide to take Rex out for his birthday on a fishing trip and they insist that he will not pay. They go on a 6-hour fishing trip with AdventureTime. How much will each of Rex's friends have to pay for the day out?

A $127.50 B $153 C $170 D $204

26 Jordan has written to the local shopping centre. She has suggested there should be more electric wheelchairs available for shoppers to borrow. The centre currently has two wheelchairs but often when Jordan's mother takes her elderly father shopping, both wheelchairs are being used and it's impossible for Jordan's father to participate in any shopping.

Which one of these statements, if true, most **weakens** Jordan's argument?

A Most people prefer to bring their own wheelchairs to the centre.

B People who have to wait for wheelchair availability might decide to shop at a different shopping centre.

C When people have to wait too long for a wheelchair they become very upset.

D Not many people know how to operate an electric wheelchair.

27 This morning I saw nine children riding in the park. Each child was riding either a bicycle or a tricycle. All of the bicycles had two wheels and all of the tricycles had three wheels. Altogether I counted 20 wheels.

How many children were riding bicycles?

A 7   B 6   C 5   D 4

28 Four sisters were asked how old their little brother was. Here are their replies.

Keira: 'He is not 5.'

Mary: 'He is 4.'

Sophie: 'He is 5.'

Alana: 'He is not 6.'

Three of the sisters were correct but one was not. Which sister got it wrong?

A Keira

B Mary

C Sophie

D Alana

☞ **Answers and explanations on pages 68–73**

29 River's family has a new car with navigation guidance. River has been asked to enter the address of the family's destination.

River: 'This car is so clever. I just need to enter the name of the street and the navigation system will tell us how to get there.'

Which one of the following sentences shows the mistake River has made?

A There are some streets which have had a change of name.

B The navigation system might not work properly.

C The destination is overseas so the car cannot drive there.

D There are streets with the same name in a number of suburbs.

30 It's common knowledge that light emitted from TV screens, tablets and smartphones will negatively impact a person's ability to sleep. The screens emit blue light, which affects our body's ability to create melatonin, the hormone that makes you feel sleepy. So stay away from blue light at night if you want to fall asleep and stay asleep!

Which one of these statements, if true, most **strengthens** the above argument?

A Some evidence suggests red, orange or yellow light is good for sleep.

B Getting enough REM (rapid eye movement) sleep helps process emotional information.

C Some lightbulbs can switch to different colours for day and night.

D Blue light in the day is a good thing because it can help a person feel more alert.

31 Jasmine had an idea for a way to reduce the sting from nettles. She mixed some ingredients and made a lotion. Later, when on a walk some friends were stung by nettles, she produced her lotion for them to try.

Jasmine drew up this table.

Name	Used Jasmine's lotion	Sting soothed
Bill	Yes	P
Daniel	Q	Yes
Ethan	No	R
Freya	S	No

Which of the missing results does Jasmine need to determine whether her lotion works?

A P and Q

B Q and R

C R and S

D P and S

32 A local community decided to hold a street party. First they surveyed the local residents to find out what activities they would prefer to have at the party.

The survey found that everyone who wanted a family fun zone also wanted a DJ. Plus anyone who wanted a DJ wanted roving performers but no-one who wanted a DJ wanted face painting.

Based on the above information, which one of the following must be true?

A If Ben wants a family fun zone, he does not want a DJ.

B If Aida does not like face painting, she does not want roving performers.

C If Finn wants a family fun zone, he does not want face painting.

D If Lola wants roving performers, she also wants a DJ.

33 The Most Improved award for Year 10 Creative Arts goes to the student who improves most in both Visual Arts and Performing Arts. The total number of extra marks achieved are added together to find the most improved. If a student's marks go down in a subject, then those marks are taken away. The marks for five students for both subjects in Years 9 and 10 are below.

Visual Arts

	Year 9	Year 10
Molly	84	89
Zach	75	72
Otis	91	91
Lonnie	69	72
Rex	74	78

Performing Arts

	Year 9	Year 10
Molly	65	70
Zach	76	85
Otis	70	79
Lonnie	73	81
Rex	85	82

Who should win the Most Improved award for Year 10 Creative Arts?

A Molly
B Zach
C Otis
D Lonnie

34 When Becky drives her car it takes 16 minutes to get from her house to the beach. When she drives three-quarters of the way to the beach, parks the car and walks the rest of the way the whole trip takes her 24 minutes.

How long would it take to walk the whole way?

A 36 minutes
B 48 minutes
C 60 minutes
D 72 minutes

35 Lisa and Jarrah attend the same karate academy. At the end of each term, their instructor gives each of her students an exam. Each student is given a score for performing an individual sequence of movements and a score for a fight match. The two scores are then added together to give a final exam score.

Lisa and Jarrah just found out that they got the same final exam score.

Lisa: 'If we each got a different score for the individual sequence, then our scores for the fight match must have been different too.'

Jarrah: 'If our individual sequence scores were the same, then our scores for the fight match must have been the same too.'

If the information in the box is true, whose reasoning is correct?

A Lisa only
B Jarrah only
C Both Lisa and Jarrah
D Neither Lisa nor Jarrah

36 If two dice are rolled and land on the same number it is said that 'a pair' has been rolled. The 'total of all dice' is the sum of the values showing on the top of the dice.

Tommy rolls five dice and gets two pairs of consecutive numbers, with the fifth dice showing a different value than the other four dice.

If the total of all dice is 16, what **must** be true?

A If he rolled a 2, he also rolled a 6.
B If he rolled a 3, he also rolled a 4.
C If he rolled a 3, he only rolled one 2.
D If he rolled a 4, he only rolled one 2.

    ☞ **Answers and explanations on pages 68–73**

37 Five children took part in a competition to find as many hidden boxes and ribbons as they could. All the children found at least one box and one ribbon and no two children found the same number of boxes; nor did any two find the same number of ribbons. No child found more than five boxes or more than five ribbons.

Daniel found four boxes and more ribbons than Niamh.

Max found the most boxes but the least number of ribbons.

Zoe found fewer ribbons than Leo but more boxes.

Leo found more boxes than Niamh but fewer ribbons.

Which one of these **cannot** be true?

A Daniel found the most ribbons.

B Niamh found the fewest boxes.

C Leo did not find exactly three ribbons.

D Zoe did not find exactly two boxes.

38 For the last 12 months the local council has been trialling the closure of a beachside street to cars. A local restaurant owner now wants the council to extend the trial. She said: 'Having the street closed to cars allows all the restaurants along the beachfront to increase their outdoor dining areas so we can have more customers.'

Which one of these statements, if true, most **weakens** the restaurant owner's claim?

A A report to Council found that pedestrian safety in the area has improved.

B A report to Council found no increase in customer numbers or spend for the beachfront businesses.

C The street closure included trialling a two-way cycleway along the beachfront.

D The Council received very polarised feedback from the community about the street closure.

39 There are two ways to qualify to enter the state skateboarding championship: by winning at least three local skateboarding competitions during the year or by breaking a state skateboarding record.

This year four students from Zara's school have qualified to enter the state skateboarding championship.

Zara: 'I know three state skateboarding records were broken this year by students from our school. So that means more than half our qualifiers must be record-breakers.'

Which one of the following sentences shows the mistake Zara has made?

A A qualifier may have broken more than one skateboarding record.

B Some qualifiers may have won more than three local skateboarding competitions.

C The number of records broken this year may be higher than in other years.

D Some qualifiers who won three local skateboarding competitions may also have broken a state record.

40   Three boys, Darcy, Huan and Oliver, and three girls, Anna, Fatima and Sara, are sitting at a rectangular table enjoying drinks.

- Three people are sitting on each of two sides of the table. Huan is enjoying a milkshake on the southern side.
- Anna is sitting at the centre of one side and is directly opposite the person who is drinking lime cordial.
- Oliver and Fatima are sitting next to each other on the same side of the table.
- Darcy is drinking orange juice and is directly opposite the person drinking cola.
- Sara is sitting next to Anna on her left.
- One of the boys is drinking water.

One person is drinking lemonade. Who is it?

A Anna
B Fatima
C Oliver
D Sara

   ☞ **Answers and explanations on pages 68–73**

SAMPLE TEST 4

1 Five children, Ali, Connor, Mo, Nathan and Zara, were collecting stickers. They all collected a different number and Zara collected the most: 32. Connor collected the least: 19. Mo collected six more than Nathan but four less than Ali.

Which **must** be true?

A Mo has 27 stickers.

B Zara has one more sticker than Ali.

C Nathan has two more stickers than Connor.

D Ali has 10 more stickers than Nathan.

2 To become a successful magician you need to practise and to invent your own tricks. You also need to have confidence in performing for members of the public.

Scarlet: 'Yoshiaki loves learning new tricks and he practises them all the time. He's always experimenting to invent new tricks. He lacks confidence at this stage but I think if he develops that, he'll be a successful magician.'

Leo: 'Isobel has amazing confidence and performs magic tricks all the time for family and friends. Sometimes the tricks don't work very well because she hasn't practised them enough but she doesn't care and neither do the audience. I'm sure she'll be a successful magician.'

If the information in the box is true, whose reasoning is correct?

A Scarlet only

B Leo only

C Both Scarlet and Leo

D Neither Scarlet nor Leo

3 Five friends, Jye, Mimi, Noah, Phoebe and Troy, live in five different towns, Jerseyville, Milton, Norwood, Palmyra and Tennyson. No person lives in a town that begins with the same initial as their own name. In addition, no two people have the same pair of initials. (If A lives in B, then B cannot live in A.)

- Troy does not live in Jerseyville.
- The person from Tennyson is not Mimi or Jye.
- Phoebe lives in Norwood.

Who comes from Palmyra?

A Jye   B Mimi

C Noah   D Troy

4 Jasmine has written a letter to the Body Corporate in her apartment building to request permission to install a black shade blind on the outer edge of her balcony to protect her unit from the westerly sun. In her letter she mentions that the Authority that mediates disputes between unit owners and their Bodies Corporate has always agreed that owners have a right to protect their homes from the sun and as long as the colour and styling of the blind complies with the building's by-laws and is installed according to safety standards and building codes, then it should be approved.

Which one of these statements, if true, **weakens** Jasmine's application?

A The by-laws allow only cream, grey or black furnishings on balconies.

B Other units in the block have all used white blinds.

C The blind will reduce the need for air conditioning in the unit and so save electricity, reducing costs and reducing the impact on the planet.

D The blind will comply with building codes, safety standards and the building's by-laws.

5 At a cake stall at the market, Brett sells his special carrot cakes for $2 each. He also sells packets of 3 for $5 and boxes of 8 for $12.

Which would be the least expensive way to buy 17 carrot cakes?

A 2 boxes of 8 and 1 single cake

B 1 box of 8 and 3 packets of 3

C 5 packets of 3 and 2 single cakes

D 17 single cakes

6 Three people are talking about a key that belongs to one of them. Each makes two statements that might or might not be true. At least one of the statements each makes is true.

Maddie says: 'This is my key. It opens a jewellery box.'

Oscar says: 'This is my key. It does not open a jewellery box.'

William says: 'This is not my key. It is Oscar's key.'

Which of the following **must** be true about the key?

A It does not belong to Oscar.

B It does not belong to William.

C It opens a jewellery box.

D It does not open a jewellery box.

7 Aiden's school was selecting students for a series of songwriting workshops run in conjunction with a well-known singer-songwriter who had volunteered her time. As well as considering students' musical ability, the school and the singer interviewed students individually and gave them a timed songwriting challenge.

If a student had proof of existing songwriting ability, then they only had to pass the interview. If they had limited proof of songwriting ability, then they had to do exceptionally well in the interview as well as the songwriting challenge.

Aiden has proof of songwriting ability but failed to be accepted for the workshops.

What must have been the reason?

A He did not do well in the songwriting challenge.

B He did well in the interview but badly in the songwriting challenge.

C He did badly in the interview.

D He had no proof of songwriting ability.

8 The International Day of Forests is a day established to focus attention on the value and significance of forests. Forests are one of our most important defences against climate change. Forests soak up carbon dioxide and store it. In theory, large-scale reforestation could absorb a third of our global emissions. In addition, many people depend on forests for their livelihoods and forests protect biodiversity. We must act now to save forests. Our future depends on it.

If the above information is true, which statement most **strengthens** the argument?

A Forests are needed to help fight climate change.

B Shinrin-yoku, or forest bathing, is a healthy activity where people walk in a forest to experience a sense of calm.

C Millions of people depend on forests for their income.

D Tropical forests contain more than half of all the world's plant and animal species.

9 Logan and Jennifer are playing a game. They begin with 25 marbles each. After the first round the loser must give the winner 1 marble. The loser must give the winner 2 marbles after the second round, 4 marbles after the third round, 8 marbles after the fourth round, and so on. The number of marbles given to the winner doubles after each round.

After 4 rounds Logan has 32 marbles, having won 3 of the 4 rounds.

Which round did Jennifer win?

A Round 1

B Round 2

C Round 3

D Round 4

☞ Answers and explanations on pages 73–79

10 The Blue Train runs between the two cities Cape Town and Pretoria. It takes 31 hours to make the trip, which includes a 1-hour stop at Kimberley, which is exactly halfway between the two cities. Once the train arrives in Pretoria from Cape Town it sits for 18 hours before making the return journey. If the train leaves Cape Town for Pretoria at 9 am on Tuesday, when will it arrive at Kimberley on its return journey to Cape Town?

A   1 am Thursday   B   2 am Thursday
C   1 am Friday   D   2 am Friday

11 To become a professional photographer you need creativity and attention to detail. Invest in your own equipment including camera, portable lighting, specialty lenses and a tripod. Learn camera operation and photo-editing skills. Practise, experiment and develop a professional portfolio.

Owen: 'Frankie has all her own equipment and she is always taking photos. She's not very organised though and has poor attention to detail. I don't think professional photography will suit her.'

Halyna: 'Adam can't afford to buy his own equipment but whenever he can, he borrows equipment and takes hundreds of photos. He's a talented photographer and photo editor and is very ambitious. He's likely to make a great professional photographer.'

If the information in the box is true, whose reasoning is correct?

A   Owen only
B   Halyna only
C   Both Owen and Halyna
D   Neither Owen nor Halyna

12 Ms Nguyen set her class a quick quiz challenge. Students had up to ten minutes to try to answer 20 quick general-knowledge quiz questions. After the quiz, five friends compared their results.

- Ying got more quiz questions correct than Eli but finished after him.
- Aziz was faster than Ying but got three quiz questions wrong.
- Lucia was not as quick to finish as Eli but Eli was not as quick as Aziz.
- Marina answered all 20 questions correctly but took the longest to finish.
- Eli finished second but got two quiz questions wrong.

If all of the above statements are true, only one of the sentences below **cannot** be true. Which one?

A   Ying got fewer quiz questions correct than Marina.
B   Aziz was faster than Lucia to finish the quiz.
C   Aziz got the fewest correct answers in the quiz.
D   Aziz was not the first to finish the quiz.

13 Two Roman generals sent coded messages to each other using a simple Caesar cipher which involves shifting the alphabet up to 26 positions. For instance, a shift of 1 position would mean A is replaced by B and B is replaced by C, C is replaced by D, and so on. A shift of 5 positions would mean A is replaced by F and B is replaced by G, and so on.

The generals decide to encrypt their messages twice before sending and indicate the two shifts that were used by writing the result of multiplying the two numbers used.

The beginning of one message reads: 18A…

Which of the following cannot be the first letter of the decrypted message?

A   R   B   H   C   S   D   P

☞ **Answers and explanations on pages 73–79**

14　Amanda has an up-to-date online directory which can be used to look up any street in the country.

Amanda: 'If you know the name of the street you want, you don't need to know which suburb it is in—you can look it up in the directory.'

If the information in the box is true, which one of the following sentences shows the mistake Amanda has made?

A　Some suburbs have changed their name.

B　Some streets have the same name as each other.

C　Some suburbs do not have any streets at all.

D　Some streets have the same name as the suburb they are in.

15　The Beachhead Volleyball Association (BVA) wants to increase the number of permanent volleyball courts on Beachhead Beach from eight to ten. The BVA argues that the increasing popularity of the sport requires extra court space. However, those using the beach for other activities say eight courts is enough.

Which one of these statements, if true, most **strengthens** the BVA's argument?

A　Other beach users do not like the messy impromptu 'courts' players set up outside the official court area.

B　The BVA has a reputation for conducting itself in a professional and cooperative manner.

C　The last time courts were added there was an agreement that there would be no more increases.

D　The popularity of beach volleyball is increasing.

16　The cog in the top left is turned in the direction of the arrow.

What will happen to the numbered weights?

A　1 and 4 will go up and 2 and 3 will go down.

B　1 and 3 will go up and 2 and 4 will go down.

C　2 and 3 will go up and 1 and 4 will go down.

D　2 and 4 will go up and 1 and 3 will go down.

17　Chloe has a new drill. The instruction manual says: 'Whenever the red light on the side of the drill is flashing on and off, it means that the motor is starting to overheat.'

Chloe: 'The motor temperature must be okay now because the red light isn't flashing at the moment.'

Malik: 'But the red light is on continuously. So that must mean that the motor has already overheated!'

If the information in the box is true, whose reasoning is correct?

A　Chloe only

B　Malik only

C　Both Chloe and Malik

D　Neither Chloe nor Malik

☞ **Answers and explanations on pages 73–79**

18 Ryan's school surveyed the Year 6 students to find out the guest speakers they would prefer to invite to speak at a special careers day. The survey found that everyone who wanted a police officer also wanted a filmmaker and everyone who wanted a filmmaker wanted a journalist, but no-one who wanted a filmmaker wanted a politician.

Based on the above information, which one of the following must be true?

A If Ryan wants a police officer, he does not want a filmmaker.

B If Tran does not want a politician, he does not want a journalist.

C If Poppy wants a police officer, she does not want a politician.

D If Suma wants a journalist, she also wants a filmmaker.

19 A special dice is to be created with a triangle, a square, a pentagon, a hexagon, a heptagon and an octagon on the faces. The number of sides of the shapes on opposite faces must sum to the same number.

Which is **not** a possible net of the dice?

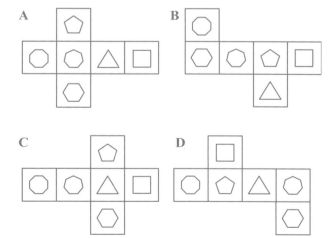

20 Seahorses are the only animal in the world where the male carries the eggs and gives birth to the young.

Asif: If you see a seahorse laying an egg, you know it must be a male.'
Daisy: 'If you see a seahorse giving birth to young seahorses, you know it can't be a female.'

If the information in the box is true, whose reasoning is correct?

A Asif only

B Daisy only

C Both Asif and Daisy

D Neither Asif nor Daisy

21 If Luca doesn't get his homework completed by 7 pm, he won't be allowed to watch the next episode of his favourite series live on TV.

If he is not able to watch the episode live, he won't be able to talk about it with his friends at school tomorrow and they might tell him what happened in the episode and spoil his enjoyment of it when he watches it on catch up.

If he can get his homework done by 7pm, he might be allowed to watch the episode live and then he can talk about it at school with his friends.

If the above statements are correct, which one of the following is **not** possible?

A Luca got his homework done by 7 pm but was not allowed to watch the episode live.

B Luca didn't get his homework done by 7 pm and was allowed to watch the episode live.

C Luca got his homework completed by 7 pm and watched the episode live.

D Luca was allowed to watch the episode live and he talked about it with his friends the next day.

SAMPLE TEST 4

22 A group of people completed a survey in which they were asked which animals they would like to have as pets. The information below was deduced from the results.

- All those who like rabbits also like dogs and cats.
- All those who like horses like dogs but nothing else.
- Fewer people like horses than like only cats.

What else must be true?

A More people like cats than the number who like horses and rabbits combined.

B More people like dogs than the number who like horses and rabbits combined.

C More people like cats than like dogs.

D More people like dogs than like cats.

23

> Deng's drama teacher has promised that any students who did not have a speaking part in last term's play will definitely be given a speaking part in this term's play.

Zihao: 'I had a speaking part in last term's play so I won't be given a speaking part in this term's play. I'm really disappointed.'

Which one of the following sentences shows the mistake Zihao has made?

A Just because anyone was not given a speaking part in the play last term, it does not mean that they would not have liked to have had one.

B Just because somebody is chosen for a speaking part, it does not mean they will actually perform in the play.

C Just because Zihao was chosen for a speaking part in the past, it does not mean he will always get a speaking part in the future.

D Just because someone who did not have a speaking part in last term's play will be given a speaking part in this term's play, it does not mean that anyone who had a speaking part last term won't be given a speaking part this term.

24 Holly and Lani both compete in a 12-lap cycling race. Lani is faster than Holly so for every two laps that Holly completes, Lani completes three laps. Lani completes the race in 10 minutes exactly. By how many minutes does she beat Holly?

A 1 minute

B 3 minutes

C 5 minutes

D 6 minutes

25 A square piece of paper is folded in half, then in half again. An inkpot drips on the paper and the ink bleeds through each layer of the paper, leaving a fainter spot on each page as it bleeds. Once the ink dries, the piece of paper is unfolded.

Which of the following is the only possible view of the unfolded paper?

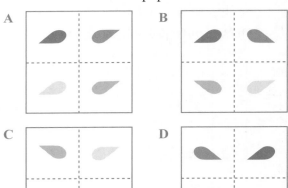

26 Fifty-three dogs live at the 45 houses in Wattle Street. Five of the houses have three dogs and 11 have two. If no houses have more than three dogs, how many houses do not have a dog?

A 16   B 15   C 14   D 13

☞ **Answers and explanations on pages 73–79**

27 In a school survey, everyone who liked art also liked drama. Everyone who liked drama liked dance, but no-one who liked drama liked choir.

David, Astrid, Isabella and Jamal all took part in the survey.

Based on the above information, which one of the following must be true?

A If David likes dance, he also likes drama.

B If Astrid does not like choir, she does not like dance.

C If Jamal likes art, he does not like choir.

D If Isabella does not like art, she does not like drama.

28 Hula dancing in Hawaii is a complex cultural and spiritual dance where every tiny movement carries meaning. Hula dancing is referred to as language in motion. Hula dances tell stories about nature, the earth, the weather and Hawaiian history. They also honour the Hawaiian gods. Children in Hawaii are encouraged to learn how to perform traditional and modern hula. There are even competitions.

Which one of the following, if true, most **strengthens** the above argument?

A Learning hula dancing is a way to pass on cultural knowledge to the next generations.

B Hula dancers tell stories through dance.

C Traditional hula is called 'Hula Kahiko' and was developed to honour and entertain the Hawaiian chiefs.

D Hula dancers train for years.

29 In a game show on television a contestant has the chance to win a prize found in one of three boxes. One box is blue, one is red and the other is green. Each box has two statements shown on it. On one box both statements are true. On another box both statements are false and the third box has one true statement and one false statement.

These are the statements:

Blue:

1. The prize is in the green box.

2. There are more wrong statements on the red box than on the green box.

Red:

1. The prize is in the blue box.

2. At least one of the statements on the green box is true.

Green:

1. Both statements on the red box are false.

2. It is a cash prize.

Which must be true?

A Both statements on the green box are false.

B It is a cash prize.

C The prize is in the red box.

D The prize is in the green box.

30 In the past if an appliance or other item broke, then people repaired it. But in our society today it is increasingly acceptable to throw out a broken item and buy a new one. Modern items are not made to last and it is cheaper to simply replace the item than to get it fixed.

Which one of these statements, if true, most **weakens** the above argument?

A Cheaply made items are not built to last.

B People like cheap goods, even if these items add to the growing waste crisis.

C Repair Cafes around the country have skilled volunteers who repair items for free.

D Our society has a deeply ingrained throwaway culture.

SAMPLE TEST 4

31 Sophie counted the number of cars of different colours that drove past her house one day. She drew a graph of the results for white, red, blue, silver and black cars, but forgot to label it.

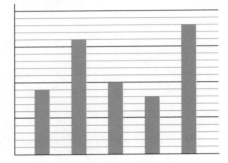

Sophie remembers that there were more white cars than cars of any other colour and the number of white cars was equal to the total of red and black cars. There were exactly half as many black cars as silver cars.

Which of these statements is **not** correct?

A There were more red cars than silver cars.

B There were fewer black cars than any of the other colours.

C There were half as many blue cars as white cars.

D There were twice as many silver and white cars together as blue and black cars combined.

32 Oliver's school was selecting students to attend a Youth Voices Forum at the local council. As well as considering a student's previous volunteer contributions to the school community, there was a teamwork assessment and a debating challenge.

If a student had made previous volunteer contributions to the school community in some way, then they only had to pass the teamwork assessment to be selected to attend. If a student had not made any previous volunteer contributions to the school community, then they either needed an excellent result in the teamwork assessment or they needed to do well in both the teamwork assessment and the debating challenge.

Oliver had previously volunteered to mentor younger students in the school but failed to be selected to attend the Youth Voices Forum. What must have been the reason?

A Oliver failed the teamwork assessment.

B Oliver did badly in the debating challenge.

C Oliver had not made any previous volunteer contributions to the school community.

D Oliver did well in the teamwork assessment but badly in the debating challenge.

33 The Most Improved Scorer award in a soccer team goes to the player who improves his goal-scoring rank among his team members by the largest number of positions.

At the end of 2021, the goal tally was:

Lionel	19
Cristiano	17
Eden	17
David	10
Romelu	7
Xabi	4
Robin	2
Lucas	0

At the end of 2022, the goal tally for the same team was:

Lionel	18
Cristiano	17
Eden	20
David	1
Romelu	5
Xabi	3
Robin	4
Lucas	2

Who won the Most Improved Scorer award?

A Eden

B Romelu

C Robin

D Lucas

☞ Answers and explanations on pages 73–79

SAMPLE TEST 4

34 A juggler throws five balls in his act. The balls continuously follow the same path through his hands and into the air. Two are black, two are white and one is yellow. If one white ball directly follows the other white ball, which statement must be true?

A The yellow ball must follow a black ball.

B One black ball must directly follow the other black ball.

C A black ball must go either directly before or after a white ball.

D The yellow ball is not directly before or after a white ball.

35 The principal at Santi's school said that any Year 6 students who did not get a chance to attend the Youth Voices Forum last year will definitely be given the chance to attend this year.

Santi: 'Oh no! I'm in Year 6 but I attended the Youth Voices Forum last year. That means I won't be allowed to attend this year. I really wanted to go again!'

Which one of the following sentences shows the mistake Santi has made?

A Just because a Year 6 student did not get a chance to attend the Youth Voices Forum last year, it does not mean that they would not have liked to attend.

B Just because any Year 6 student who did not get a chance to attend the Youth Voices Forum last year will be given a chance to attend this year, it does not mean that any Year 6 student who attended last year will not be able to attend again this year.

C Just because Santi attended the Youth Voices Forum last year, it does not mean that he will be selected to attend this year.

D Just because a Year 6 student did not get a chance to attend the Youth Voices Forum last year, it does not mean that they will be given a chance to attend this year.

36 Here are the first four steps in a pattern.

Which step comes next?

A ■ ⬠ ◆ ✦ ● ▼

B ■ ◆ ✦ ⬠ ● ▼

C ● ▼ ⬠ ◆ ✦ ■

D ● ▼ ✦ ⬠ ◆ ■

37 A community op shop gave out five grants to local organisations. These went to the sea scouts, the tennis club, the pony club, the cricket club and the men's shed.

■ The pony club and the sea scouts received the same amount.

■ The cricket club received $2000 less than the pony club.

■ The tennis club received a larger grant than the pony club but less than the men's shed.

■ The sea scouts received $5000.

■ The men's shed received $6000 more than the cricket club.

Which of the following statements must be true?

A The tennis club received $8000.

B The men's shed received $3000 more than the sea scouts.

C All the grants were less than $10 000.

D The cricket club did not receive the least amount.

38 Tim's father is an entomologist researching the sustainability of insect farming. He says: 'Insects are not only gaining attention as a sustainable source of protein in our diet, they could also be nutritionally beneficial to our plants.'

Which one of these statements, if true, most **strengthens** Tim's father's argument?

A Eighty per cent of the world's population is already eating insects but in some countries people are still squeamish about this.

B Farming insects is more sustainable than farming meat.

C Insect poo is called frass.

D Exoskeletons discarded when insects moult can provide excellent nutrition for plant growth when added to the soil.

39 Researchers have found that some fish species communicate by making noises. Herring find each other in the dark by using high-pitched farts. Clownfish warn intruders by clacking their jaws together. But the three-spined toadfish is the only fish known to cry like a baby.

Xavier: 'If you hear a fish crying like a baby, you know it must be a three-spined toadfish.'

Melia: 'And if you hear an underwater animal crying like a baby, and you know it isn't a three-spined toadfish, then it can't be a fish.'

If the information in the box is true, whose reasoning is correct?

A Xavier only

B Melia only

C Both Xavier and Melia

D Neither Xavier nor Melia

40 Five people, Milly, Aaron, Luke, Fahad and Beth, work at an insurance company. They have offices all in a row and those offices are numbered from 1 to 5.

1	2	3	4	5

Fahad's office is somewhere between Luke's and Milly's.

Aaron's office is a higher number than Fahad's but lower than Beth's.

Milly's office is a higher number than Luke's but lower than Aaron's.

Who has office number 3?

A Milly

B Aaron

C Luke

D Fahad

1 Bonnie, Darcy, Hannah, Jeremy, Leonie and Tyson are neighbours. Their ages, in ascending order, are 4, 5, 7, 9, 10 and 12.

- Leonie is older than Jeremy but younger than Hannah.
- Darcy is older than Bonnie but younger than Tyson.
- The sum of the ages of Bonnie and Hannah is twice that of Darcy.

Who is 9 years old?

A Darcy

B Jeremy

C Leonie

D Bonnie

2 Button batteries are small and round. They are often used in remote controls, cameras, toys, musical greeting cards and watches. Young children are sometimes tempted to put them in their mouths and may accidently swallow them. Some children even put them up their nose or in their ears where they can cause burns or even death. A flat battery can harm children too if swallowed as it will still have some charge left. Keep items with button batteries in them away from small children or make sure you buy items where the battery compartments are inaccessible to small fingers.

Charlotte: 'We have lots of things that use button batteries but my two-year-old sister can't open them yet. We've seen her try when we leave the remotes on the coffee table. We only buy button batteries in packaging that needs to be cut open with scissors. She can't use scissors yet so she's safe.'

Austin: 'The back of our air-conditioning remote control pops off when the control is dropped on the floor. Then the battery is exposed. We have to quickly grab it before my brother gets to it. He thinks it's a great game but we're always faster than him. He's a toddler so he's slow and not at risk.'

If the information in the box is true, whose reasoning is correct?

A Charlotte only

B Austin only

C Neither Charlotte nor Austin

D Both Charlotte and Austin

3 Jacob has these three different shapes.

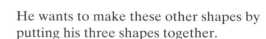

He wants to make these other shapes by putting his three shapes together.

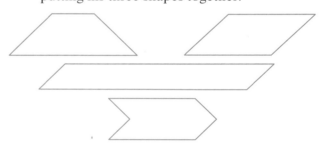

How many of these can Jacob make by placing his three shapes together?

A 1   B 2   C 3   D 4

4 A car is faster than a truck so that it takes the car 2 hours to complete a journey that it takes the truck 3 hours to complete. If the two vehicles leave Town A for Town B at 7 am and the truck arrives at 11 am, what time will the car arrive?

A 8:20 am

B 9:40 am

C 10 am

D 1 pm

5 Jo, Felix and Meg each have 25 marbles and are playing a game. They take it in turns to spin this spinner:

If the spinner lands on an even number, the player must give that number of marbles to each of the other players. If the spinner lands on an odd number, the player receives that number of marbles from each of the other players. If the spinner lands on the star, no marbles are won or lost.

In the first round, Jo goes first and spins a 2. Felix then spins a 3. Meg's spin lands on the star.

In the second round, Jo spins 3 and Felix spins 1.

After the second round, Jo has 27 marbles and Felix has 36.

What did Meg spin on her second spin?

A 4 B 3 C 2 D 1

6 Alerting devices are used by people who are hearing or sight impaired. One such device is a bed shaker, which vibrates to raise an alert for the hearing impaired. This small device can be placed under the pillow at night. It is wirelessly connected to a smoke alarm so if the smoke alarm goes off, the bed shaker will vibrate strongly and wake the sleeper. Bed shakers are life-saving devices.

Which one of these statements, if true, most **strengthens** the above argument?

A Bed shakers are especially invaluable for hearing-impaired people who live alone.

B Smoke alarms detect smoke and therefore potentially a fire.

C Some bed shakers also use strobe lighting for people who are hearing but not vision impaired.

D People who are hearing impaired cannot hear smoke alarms.

7 Nigel is at a market and wants to buy some pies. He notices that four different stallholders are selling pies but all have different prices and special offers.

Stallholder	Normal price per pie	Special offer
Gaynor	$5.50	Buy 2 get 1 free
Sandra	$5	Buy 3 get 1 free
Holly	$4.40	Buy 2 get the third for half price
Joanne	$4	Buy 3 get the fourth for half price

From which stallholder can Nigel buy 12 pies for the least amount?

A Gaynor
B Sandra
C Holly
D Joanne

8 To test his students' reasoning skills a teacher made three statements. Each of the statements was made up of two parts and at least one of the parts was true.

The statements were:

■ I was born in England but have lived in Australia since I was five.

■ I was not born in New Zealand; I was born in Canada.

■ I was born in England and moved to Australia when I was seven.

Which must be true?

A He was born in Canada.
B He was born in England.
C He has lived in Australia since he was five.
D He moved to Australia when he was seven.

9 Whoever is chosen as lead actor for the next musical at the local amateur theatre must have both singing talent and time to rehearse.

If this is true, which one of these sentences must be true?

A If Louis is not chosen as lead actor, he cannot have had the talent.

B If Louis has both talent and time to rehearse, he must be chosen as lead actor.

C If Louis is not chosen as lead actor, he must not have the time to rehearse.

D If Louis does not have time to rehearse, he cannot be the lead actor.

10 In a parent survey at a primary school, all parents who wanted their children to participate in computer classes also wanted them to learn Japanese. All parents who wanted their children to learn Japanese also wanted them to learn to play a musical instrument, but no parents who wanted their child to learn Japanese cared about their child joining the chess club.

Alice, Vince, Myra and Simon all took part in the survey.

Based on the above information, which one of the following must be true?

A If Vince supported learning a musical instrument, he also supported learning Japanese.

B If Alice did not support chess, she did not support musical instruments.

C If Myra supported computer lessons, she did not support the Chess Club.

D If Simon did not support computer lessons, he did not support learning Japanese.

11 When Melani told Josh she was going to make a playlist to listen to on the way to the exam, Josh said: 'You should search for music that plays at 60 beats per minute. That's the best tempo for encouraging alpha brainwaves.'

Which one of these statements, if true, most **strengthens** Josh's argument?

A Listening to your favourite music can boost your mood.

B Alpha brainwaves signal a calm and focused mind.

C Both meditation and exercise increase alpha brainwaves.

D Researchers have studied how to manipulate brainwaves for a better mental state.

12 Ms Street said: 'Whoever was elected Patrol Leader must have been both approved by the Scoutmaster and ranked Second Class or higher.'

If this is true, which one of these sentences must also be true?

A If Oscar was not elected Patrol Leader, he must not have been ranked Second Class or higher.

B If Talia was both approved by the Scoutmaster and ranked Second Class or higher, she must have been elected Patrol Leader.

C If Locky was not elected Patrol Leader, he must not have been approved by the Scoutmaster.

D If Ruby was not ranked Second Class or higher, she cannot have been elected Patrol Leader.

13 Gerard used a simple cipher to encrypt a message to his friend. The cipher is shown below.

A	B	C	D	E	F	G	H	I	J	K	L	M
Z	Y	X	W	V	U	T	S	R	Q	P	O	N
N	O	P	Q	R	S	T	U	V	W	X	Y	Z
M	L	K	J	I	H	G	F	E	D	C	B	A

So, to write HELLO, Gerard would write SVOOL.

Gerard's friend Heather decided to create a similar cipher but treated the alphabet as two separate 13-letter blocks of letters.

Heather wanted to write GREAT. What would she have written?

A FIBBY   B GVIMT

C TVIMG   D TIVZG

14

To become a successful entomologist, you need to be comfortable handling insects and also have excellent observational skills.

Faisal: 'Luna loves insects! She keeps pet cockroaches and picked one up with her bare hands to show me! She's always talking about how she observes them behaving and what kind of environment they need. She'd be a successful entomologist for sure.'

Sophie: 'Harry loves insects too. He's really good at finding them when we go on bushwalks. He seems to know just where to look. And he can tell you all about them. But he doesn't seem to like handling them. So he probably wouldn't be a successful entomologist.'

If the information in the box is true, whose reasoning is correct?

A Faisal only

B Sophie only

C Both Faisal and Sophie

D Neither Faisal nor Sophie

15 The local council has received an application from Friends of Deep Creek Reserve to rename it Irene Blake Reserve. The proposal aims to recognise the contribution made by Irene Blake to saving the reserve from private development as a row of townhouses. Tim Smith opposes the application. He says: 'Deep Creek Reserve has a long history in the community and is well known and loved by that name. The name should not be changed or we will lose our history.'

Which one of these statements, if true, most **weakens** Tim Smith's argument?

A Deep Creek Reserve was named five years ago after the townhouse development was cancelled.

B The proposal is consistent with Council's policy for the naming of reserves and other facilities.

C The Council has invited public submissions for and against the proposal.

D Not all members of the Friends of Deep Creek Reserve agree with the proposal to change the name.

16

David's teacher told the class: 'There are two ways to qualify to enter the State Poetry Slam being held next term: by entering at least three local poetry competitions in the last year or by winning one previous competition.'

This year six students from David's school have qualified to enter the State Poetry Slam.

David: 'I know that four poetry competitions were won in the last year by students from our school. So that means that more than half of our qualifiers must be competition winners.'

Which one of the following sentences shows the mistake David has made?

A A qualifier may have won more than one poetry competition.

B Some qualifiers may have entered more than three local poetry competitions in the last year.

C The number of poetry competitions this year may be higher than in other years.

D Some qualifiers who entered three local poetry competitions may also have won a competition.

17 The cog in the top left is turned in the direction of the arrow.

What will happen to the numbered weights?

A 1 and 4 will go up and 2 and 3 will go down.

B 1 and 3 will go up and 2 and 4 will go down.

C 2 and 3 will go up and 1 and 4 will go down.

D 2 and 4 will go up and 1 and 3 will go down.

18 If Dora does not go to training, then she likely won't be prepared for the big game on Saturday.

If she isn't prepared, then she will not play well in the game on Saturday.

If she plays well in the game on Saturday, then she might be offered a place in the Zone team.

Otherwise there is no way she will be offered a place in the Zone team.

Based on the above information, which one of the following **cannot** be true?

A Dora did not go to training but she was offered a place in the Zone team.

B Dora went to training but she was not offered a place in the Zone team.

C Dora was not prepared but she was offered a place in the Zone team.

D Dora was prepared but she was not offered a place in the Zone team.

19 The following net is folded into a six-faced dice.

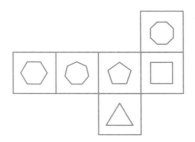

In a game, a player rolls this dice and a score is calculated by multiplying the number of sides of the shape facing upwards with the number of sides of the shape exactly opposite it (the one face down on the table). What is the difference between the minimum and maximum scores?

A 6

B 4

C 2

D no difference

20 Arlo's school surveyed the students to find out how they felt about potential names for the new music room that had just been built. The survey found that everyone who liked Tune Room also liked Mozart Room. Everyone who liked Mozart Room liked Music Room, but no-one who liked Mozart Room liked Rap Room.

Based on the above information, which one of the following must be true?

A If Arlo likes Tune Room, he does not like Mozart Room.

B If Mimi does not like Rap Room, she does not like Music Room.

C If Sofie likes Music Room, she also likes Mozart Room

D If Ilkay likes Tune Room, he does not like Rap Room.

21 Ms Lee divided the class into five groups. Each group had to build a bridge and then check to see how many toy cars it could hold without collapsing.

■ Group one was faster at building its bridge than group four but the bridge only held two cars before it collapsed.

■ Group two's bridge held five cars before collapsing but took the longest to build.

■ Group three built its bridge the second fastest and the bridge held three cars before collapsing

■ Group four's bridge held more cars than group three's bridge but it took longer to build than group three's.

■ Group five wasn't as fast to build its bridge as group three but group three was not as fast as group one.

If all the above statements are true, only one of the sentences below **cannot** be true. Which one?

A Group four's bridge held fewer cars than group two's bridge.

B Group one built their bridge faster than group five built theirs.

C Group one was not the first group to finish building their bridge.

D Group one's bridge collapsed with the fewest cars.

22 A group of students were asked which pizza toppings they liked out of four options. Students could pick more than one topping, but must choose at least one.

■ All those who liked Meatlovers also liked Supreme.

■ All those who liked Supreme also liked Hawaiian.

■ None of those who liked Vegetarian liked Meatlovers.

■ Some of those who liked Supreme liked Vegetarian.

Jin, Colin, Sophie and Amanda all took part in the survey.

Based on the above information, which of the following must be true?

A If Jin doesn't like Vegetarian, he must like Meatlovers.

B If Colin likes Supreme and Vegetarian, he must like Hawaiian.

C If Sophie likes Supreme, she must like Meatlovers.

D If Amanda doesn't like Supreme, she must not like Vegetarian.

23
> When Evie saw an ad for a fun painting workshop being held on the weekend, she asked her friend Isaac if he wanted to go with her.

Isaac: 'I'm too stressed. I wouldn't be able to concentrate on painting. I just want to relax and try to sleep!'

Evie: 'The workshop only goes for a few hours so you'll still have plenty of time to sleep! And the break will help you relax and not feel so stressed.'

Which one of these statements, if true, most **strengthens** Evie's argument?

A Research shows that creative activities reduce stress levels.

B The workshop leader is a famous artist.

C The workshop is part of a local festival and participation is free.

D A new study suggests people should get at least eight hours sleep each night.

24 To access my computer, a six-digit code must be entered.

- The first and sixth digits are the same.
- The fifth digit is three times the second digit.
- The two-digit number formed by the last two digits of the code is found by multiplying the first digit by the two-digit number made by the middle two digits.

If the first digit is 4, what is the fourth digit?

A 1   B 2   C 4   D 6

25 Felix and Olivia each have a vegetable garden. This year they each entered a tomato in the competition at their gardening club's spring fair. In the tomato competition each entry is given a score for size and a score for taste. The two scores are then added together to give a final score.

Felix and Olivia just found out that their tomatoes got the same final score.

Felix: 'If our tomatoes each got a different score for size, then their scores for taste must have been different too.'

Olivia: 'If our tomato size scores were the same, then their scores for taste must have been the same too.'

If the information in the box is true, whose reasoning is correct?

A Felix only

B Olivia only

C Both Felix and Olivia

D Neither Felix nor Olivia

26 Four boys, Billy, Elijah, Henry and Patrick, are playing a game. Each boy has counters in a different colour from the others. The counters are red, green, blue and yellow. When asked what colour they were using, each made two separate statements.

Billy: 'I have blue. Henry has green.'

Elijah: 'I have yellow. Billy has red.'

Henry: 'I have red. Patrick has blue.'

Patrick: 'I have green. Henry has blue.'

None of the statements were correct. What colour counters does Billy have?

A red

B green

C blue

D yellow

27 The local council is considering naming the new enclosed off-leash dog area at Dusty Creek War Memorial Playing Fields the Purple Poppy Dog Park and has invited the community to have their say.

The owner of the gym next door to the playing fields said: 'Brave servicemen and women gave their lives to protect our country. We should not insult them by naming a dog park 'poppy'—the red poppy is a symbol of that sacrifice and should be respected.'

Which one of these statements, if true, most **weakens** the gym owner's claim?

A The purple poppy commemorates the deeds of animals in wartime.

B The purple poppy is worn alongside the traditional red poppy.

C The new dog park has a section with an agility course to exercise dogs and a special dog-wash bay.

D The Dusty Creek RSL (Returned and Services League) proposed the name to honour the animals who served alongside their members.

28 Jordan has these three pieces of card.

How many of these shapes can he make with his pieces of card?

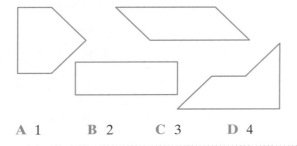

A 1   **B** 2   **C** 3   **D** 4

29 The students in a class were asked to draw a picture graph to show the information in this table.

Birds counted per sector	
Sector	**Number of birds**
North	30
East	32
South	22
West	24

One boy took so long to draw the birds that he used as symbols that he didn't get the graph finished. He did have the right number of symbols for the sectors he used but he still had one sector to draw and he needed to label his graph and add a key. The order of the sectors used is not necessarily the same as the order in the table.

Which sector did the boy still have to draw?
A North   **B** East   **C** South   **D** West

30 Bree volunteers at the zoo every weekend. Her supervisor has promised that any volunteers who did not have a chance to work in the penguin enclosure on the last roster will definitely be chosen to work in the penguin enclosure on the next roster.

Bree: 'Oh no! Penguins are my favourite. But I worked in the penguin enclosure on the last roster. So that means I definitely won't be chosen to work there on the next roster.'

Which one of the following sentences shows the mistake Bree has made?

A Just because a volunteer did not get a chance to work in the penguin enclosure on the last roster, it does not mean that they would not have liked to work there.

B Just because a volunteer who did not get a chance to work in the penguin enclosure on the last roster will be chosen to work there on the next roster, it does not mean that a volunteer who worked in the penguin enclosure on the last roster will not be able to work there again next roster.

C Just because Bree worked in the penguin enclosure last roster, it does not mean that she will be chosen to work there this roster.

D Just because a volunteer did not get a chance to work in the penguin enclosure on the last roster, it does not mean that they will be given a chance to work there next roster.

31 A square piece of paper is folded in half, then in half again. A shape is drawn in permanent marker on the paper so that the ink bleeds through all paper beneath. The folded piece of paper looks like this:

Which is the only possible view of the unfolded paper?

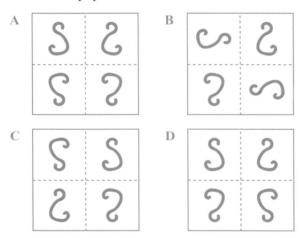

32 Logan's school was selecting stories for the yearbook. As well as considering whether a student was in the Writing Club, the yearbook committee set a word-count limit and also gave students a list of preferred writing topics. The committee also gave each story a score for grammar and spelling.

If a student was in the Writing Club, then their story only had to be within the word-count limit to be selected. If a student was not in the Writing Club, then they either needed an excellent grammar and spelling score, or they needed a good grammar and spelling score for a story about a preferred topic.

Logan was in the Writing Club but his story was not selected for the yearbook. What must have been the reason?

A His story received a bad score for spelling and grammar.

B His story was outside the word-count limit.

C He was not in the Writing Club.

D His story was not about a preferred topic.

33 Six empty seats are evenly spaced around a circular table. Albie, Bertie, Camilla, Diana, Eddie and Fred are to sit at the table. Albie sits down first. As a group, the other people walk around the table in a clockwise direction from Albie to take their seats. Bertie sits in the second empty seat after Albie. Camilla sits in the second empty seat after Bertie. This continues, as each person skips the first empty seat they come to and sits in the second empty seat after the person who just sat down. Diana sits down next, followed by Eddie and then Fred is the last to take his seat.

From Albie's perspective, who is seated directly on his right-hand side?

A Camilla

B Diana

C Eddie

D Fred

34 Five coloured boxes are placed on a table in front of Gina, who is blindfolded. Inside one of the boxes is a pair of scissors to cut off the blindfold. She can touch all the boxes but can only open one. A number of clues are read to her before she makes her choice.

- The scissors are in a box next to the green box.
- The scissors are not in the middle box.
- The pink box is next to the white box.
- The red box is 2 spaces from the blue box.
- The blue box is 3 spaces from the pink box.
- The white box is farthest left.

Which box should Gina open?

A the box farthest left

B the box farthest right

C the box second from the left

D the box second from the right

35 A nutritionist claims: 'We all know that a healthy diet is critical to your immune system. A strong immune system is one of the best defences against infection. Studies show that microgreens, tiny baby vegetables, are an important catalyst to driving immunity at a cellular level. Microgreens have the ability to activate the production of powerful antioxidants within our cells. These antioxidants decrease cell damage, which in turn can help fight disease. Microgreens are the most nutritious foods you can eat to boost your immune system.'

Which one of these statements, if true, most **strengthens** the nutritionist's argument?

A Cruciferous vegetables, such as broccoli, boost production of antioxidants.

B Microgreens produce 100 times more antioxidants than mature vegetables.

C Microgreens are a nutritious food and will boost your immune system through the production of antioxidants.

D Antioxidants can help fight disease.

36 Train A leaves Sydney for Newcastle at 1 pm and arrives at 3 pm. Train B is only half as fast as Train A and leaves Newcastle for Sydney at 2 pm.

At what time will they pass each other?

A 2:20 pm

B 2:30 pm

C 2:40 pm

D 2:45 pm

37 A farmer has 162 cows and they have a total of 98 calves. Eight of the cows have twin calves. Of the remaining cows, some have one calf and the remainder do not yet have a calf. How many of the cows do not have a calf?

A 72

B 80

C 82

D 90

38 Four people, Luisa, Isaac, Chung and Lily, are waiting in a line at the local shop. Each is buying a different item (bread, eggs, meat or milk) and each has a different-coloured bag in which to put their purchase.

■ The person with the green bag, who is first in line, is buying milk.

■ Chung is somewhere behind Isaac and immediately in front of the person buying eggs.

■ Lily is directly behind the person with the red bag.

■ Luisa, who has the blue bag, is not buying meat.

Who is buying bread?

A Luisa

B Isaac

C Chung

D Lily

39 | The only invertebrates that have wings are insects.

Alice: 'If you see an animal with wings and you know it isn't an insect, then it can't be an invertebrate.'

Marcus: 'And if you see an animal without wings and you know it is an invertebrate, then it can't be an insect.'

If the information in the box is true, whose reasoning is correct?

A Alice only

B Marcus only

C Both Alice and Marcus

D Neither Alice nor Marcus

☞ **Answers and explanations on pages 79–85**

40 Eman entered a painting in a local art competition. Entrants to the competition are allowed to enter only one painting.

Mum: 'Judges score the paintings and award prizes for first, second and third. Plus there is also a special prize for best use of imagery from the local area.'

Eman: 'So that means four entrants will get prizes.'

Which one of the following sentences shows the mistake Eman has made?

A One entrant might be awarded a prize for more than one painting.

B Some paintings might be disqualified.

C We don't know how many paintings will be entered in the competition.

D The special prizewinner might also come first, second or third.

SAMPLE TEST 1

Page 4

1 A 2 D 3 D 4 B 5 B 6 D 7 B 8 B 9 A
10 C 11 C 12 C 13 A 14 A 15 D 16 D
17 C 18 B 19 C 20 B 21 C 22 A 23 D
24 A 25 D 26 A 27 D 28 C 29 D 30 C
31 B 32 D 33 B 34 B 35 B 36 C 37 C
38 A 39 D 40 A

1 Buttercup and Pansy are the same age so they are both 2 weeks older than Poppy, who is 1 week older than Daisy. So Buttercup and Pansy are 3 weeks older than Daisy. Bluebell is 4 weeks older than Daisy so Bluebell is 1 week older than Buttercup and Pansy.

Bluebell is the oldest and Daisy the youngest. Buttercup is 3 weeks older than Daisy but 1 week younger than Bluebell, not 2.

2 The information tells you that if Heike can't visit her friends on Saturday, she will miss out on planning for Gabi's birthday celebration. It is not possible that Heike was not allowed to visit her friends but still helped plan for the party.

The other options are incorrect. These outcomes are all possible given the information in the statements.

3 Alice can be placed in any position with Cara opposite her. Paige is next to Alice. Jess is opposite Paige so she must be next to Cara. Susie is on Jess's right so Cara must be on Jess's left.

This means that Jess is sitting on Cara's right, Susie is on Alice's left and Paige is on Alice's right.

The remaining spot is on Cara's left and this must be for Victoria.

4 The oldest child must pay adult price so there are 6 people who are classed as adults. The lowest price they can pay is a family ticket plus a couple ticket: $25 + $15 = $40.

The youngest child can go free. The other four children must pay half the adult single price. Half of $10 is $5 and 4 × $5 = $20.

The lowest total price is $40 + $20 ($60).

5 The argument is that commercial fishing, especially gillnet fishing, should not be allowed near sea-lion colonies because sea lions get caught in the nets and drown. This argument is strengthened by the statement that numbers of sea-lion pups born each year are declining. If sea-lion numbers are declining anyway, any death caused by gillnets will further reduce the population.

A is incorrect. This statement might be true but it does not strengthen the argument against commercial fishing near sea-lion colonies.

C is incorrect. This statement might be true but it does not add further evidence to strengthen the argument.

D is incorrect. This is an argument to support banning gillnet fishing in general but is not specific to gillnet fishing near sea-lion colonies.

6 13 June is a Sunday. So the Sundays in June will be 6, 13, 20 and 27. 4 June will be a Friday. The play is being performed on 6 nights each week. The extra afternoon performance on Saturdays means there will be 7 performances each week. From Friday 4 June to Thursday 24 June is 3 weeks. So that means there will be 3 × 7 or 21 performances. There is also the charity performance on 13 June and a performance on Friday 25, 2 on Saturday 26 and 1 on Sunday 27. That means there will be 26 performances altogether.

7 The digits 1, 2, 7, 8 and 9 are all used. The missing four digits are four of the five digits 0, 3, 4, 5 and 6.

The units column adds to 8 (it cannot be 18 or 28). The two missing digits in the units column must add to 6 so they can only be 0 and 6. The tens column must then add to 17. The two missing numbers must add to 8. They can only be 3 and 5.

The digit that is not used is 4. The sum will be one of these:

56	30	50	36
30	56	36	50
+92	+92	+92	+92
178	178	178	178

8 Grace has not realised people might buy more than one raffle ticket and could therefore possibly win more than one raffle prize. A raffle prize winner might also win the lucky door prize.

A is incorrect. This might be true but is not the mistake Grace has made.

C is incorrect. This is neither true nor the mistake Grace has made.

D is incorrect. This is true but is not the mistake Grace has made.

9 If it is true that whoever stole the T-shirts must have had a motive, it must also be true that if Noel did not steal the T-shirts, he cannot have had a motive.

B is incorrect. Just because Noel had an opportunity to steal the T-shirts does not mean he must have stolen them.

C and D are incorrect. These sentences don't make logical sense.

10 The positioning of the circular indentation must be on the section that does not extend the full width of the cube. This means the answer must be C or D. C is the one that will rotate to fit with the original shape, while D is a reflection of C and in this case will not fit.

11 Jack uses correct reasoning. If Jack and Flynn got different scores for attitude but the same overall score, in order for their overall score to be the same their scores for performance must have also been different.

Flynn uses correct reasoning. If Jack and Flynn got the same overall score and they know their scores for attitude were the same, they must have got the same score for performance too.

The other options are incorrect by a process of elimination.

12 Since Bella was nominated by a teacher, the result of the interview was not relevant in her case. She only had to pass the school-service challenge in order to attend the leadership conference. Since she was not selected to attend, she must have failed the school-service challenge.

A is incorrect. This statement might be true. However, since Bella was nominated by a teacher, the result of the interview was not relevant in her case. So this cannot be the reason she was not selected.

B is incorrect. The information tells us Bella was nominated by a teacher.

D is incorrect. Since Bella was nominated by a teacher she only had to pass the school-service challenge in order to be selected to attend the conference. So the statement that she did well in the challenge cannot be true since Bella failed to be selected. Since it cannot be true this cannot be the reason.

13 If the back wheel of the bike turns a full revolution in the same time, then bikes 3 and 4 will move further than bikes 1 and 2 in that time as the diameter of the wheel is bigger. So D is true.

If the back wheel of two bikes is the same size, then they will move the same distance in that time, meaning they travel at the same speed. So C is true.

Louis is riding bike 4. His back wheel is large, while his front wheel is small. When his back wheel makes a full rotation, his front wheel will make more than one rotation. No-one else's bike will have a front wheel turning faster than the back wheel. So B is true.

The opposite is true for Gloria's bike. Her front wheel is turning slower than her back wheel. A is not true.

14 This statement is further evidence to support Daisy's argument that the Skate Park provides significant benefits for the whole community and so most strengthens that argument.

B and C are incorrect. These statements provide extra information about why the Council is considering closing the Skate Park but do not strengthen Daisy's argument about the benefits of the Skate Park.

D is incorrect. This is a restatement of a comment Daisy has already made so it doesn't strengthen the argument.

15 Neither Hudson's nor Dylan's reasoning is correct. Hudson's reasoning that all the tyres must be correct is flawed. The manual says the warning light comes on when the tyre pressure is **too** low. Therefore one or more of the tyres might still not have the correct pressure but the pressure might not yet be low enough to register as too low and set off the warning light. Dylan's reasoning that the tyres are all okay and the light won't come on because he checked the tyres last week is also flawed. Just because he checked the tyres last week does not mean something won't have happened to cause the tyres to lose pressure since then. Also, even if the tyres are all okay, the manual says the light might come in if there is a fault in the system.

The other options are incorrect by a process of elimination.

16 High ropes can only be chosen in Session 4. This means that Archery must be chosen in Session 3 as it cannot be chosen in Session 4. This means that Woodcarving must be chosen in Session 1 as it cannot be chosen in Session 3. Sienna must now choose an activity for Session 2. Orienteering is not on that list so cannot be chosen.

17 From the information given you can draw the conclusion that if Leo's parents are unhappy, there is no way they will let him go to the party. So this conclusion is not possible.

A is incorrect. This statement might be true. Even though Leo did not study, he might still have passed the test and made his parents happy. If they were happy, they might have let him go to the party.

B is incorrect. This statement might be true. Leo might have studied but still failed the test. Or he might have studied and passed the test but his parents still did not let him go to the party.

D is incorrect. This statement might be true. The information tells us that if Leo's parents are happy, they might let him go to the party—not that they will definitely let him go.

18 To come to the conclusion that four entrants will get ribbons, Willow has added the one ribbon for People's Choice to the three ribbons for first, second and third. She has then assumed the four ribbons will go to four different entrants. She has not considered that the People's Choice winner might also come first, second or third—and therefore will receive two of the ribbons, meaning only three entrants might get ribbons.

A is incorrect. The information tells us that each entrant can only enter one arrangement. So this sentence shows a mistake, although it is not a mistake Willow has made.

C and D are incorrect. These statements might be true but do not impact the number of ribbons awarded and are not mistakes Willow has made.

19 All those who like soccer like Aussie Rules. So it follows that if Hala likes soccer, she must like Aussie Rules.

20 Emma is correct to reason that the expression 'waste not want not' means if you conserve resources and aren't wasteful, you will never be in need.

A is incorrect. This statement does not make sense.

C is incorrect. The expression is more general than wanting one wasted thing back and its intention is to encourage people not to be wasteful in general.

D is incorrect. The reasoning in this explanation does not make sense.

21 If the person who removed the fire extinguisher from the foyer wall needed to have a motive, then someone without a motive cannot have removed it.

A is incorrect. Wan would not have removed it without a motive.

B is incorrect. This statement is not logical.

D is incorrect. Just because Wan had a motive and an opportunity does not mean she removed the fire extinguisher.

22 In this diagram, each grid square is 100 m wide.

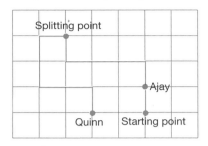

The walk from the starting point to the lookout is 600 m so if Ajay walks back 500 m on that track, he is only 100 m north of the starting point and must continue to walk 100 m in a southerly direction. Quinn ends up 200 m west of the starting point so must walk in an easterly direction.

23 Alan uses flawed reasoning. The Hawksbill sea turtle does not produce a venom to inject into its prey. It is poisonous to eat but not venomous.

The other options are incorrect. The reasoning in these statements is correct.

24 The argument is that seahorses face a grim future. The evidence lists numerous reasons for this. Any statement which adds an extra reason for describing the seahorse's future as grim will strengthen the argument. This statement adds the additional evidence that seahorse deaths are sometimes the result of trawler by-catch.

The other options are incorrect. These statements are all ways to support seahorse survival but not further evidence of the problems they face.

25 We don't know any of the distances between the towns. However, looking at the two diagrams we can see some possible arrangements.

If Town A is due west of Town B, they will always be on the same horizontal line in a grid. Town C is below Town A. Town D, being south-east of Town C, will always be below the level of Town C on a grid and must also be directly south of Town B.

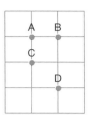 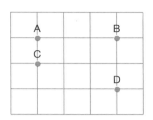

The distance between Town A and Town C will **always** be shorter than the distance between Town B and Town D. So the answer is D.

26 The shape is a square. One of the outer pieces is 3 squares wide and 7 squares long so the square must also be 7 squares wide. The piece that is 4 squares long must join with that piece. The final outer piece can then be added. The missing inner piece must then have two squares on two adjoining sides. It must be the piece in option A.

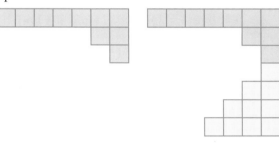

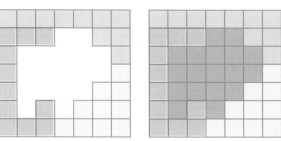

27 Number the five positions from 1 to 5. The portrait is on the far left so is in position 1 and the landscape is in the centre (position 3). Bill's seascape cannot be in position 2 because that would mean that the still life and photograph would be next to each other in positions 4 and 5. So the seascape is in either position 4 or 5 and Farid's artwork is next to it in either position 5 or 4 (as it is not the landscape).

Vic's work is somewhere to the right of Dane's and to the left of Abe's. So the portrait belongs to Dane in position 1, Vic's work is in position 2 and Abe has the landscape in position 3. The photograph is not next to Dane's work so the artwork in position 2 can only be the still life. It is the work of Vic.

28 The argument is that Auslan should be taught in all schools. The statement that weakens the argument is that there are only 30 000 hearing impaired people who use Auslan in Australia.

A is incorrect. This statement is irrelevant to an argument to teach Auslan in schools but it does provide a reason why Auslan is not taught in more schools.

B is incorrect. This statement strengthens the need to teach Auslan to more people.

D is incorrect. This statement strengthens the argument to teach Auslan in school.

29 David rolls a 3 so must give 3 counters to Isabel and 3 counters to Julia. So after David's roll he has 14 counters, and Isabel and Julia both have 23.

Isabel then rolls a 1 and must give a counter to David and a counter to Julia. David then has 15 counters, Isabel has 21 and Julia has 24.

After Julia's roll David has 9 counters so he has lost 6 counters. Julia must have rolled a 6 and received 6 counters from each of David and Isabel. So Julia has 24 + 6 + 6 or 36 counters.

30 This statement provides evidence that butterfly populations are in trouble and need our help and so most strengthens the argument to leave caterpillars in the garden.

A is incorrect. It provides extra information about butterflies but does not strengthen the argument about leaving caterpillars in the garden.

B is incorrect. It provides a reason to enjoy watching caterpillars but does not **most** strengthen the argument.

D is incorrect. It supports the argument but does not **most** strengthen it.

31 Zoe and Ray made contradictory statements so one of them must have been lying and Tarek must have told the truth. The person who broke the vase wasn't Zoe; it was Ray.

32 Neither Summer nor Jack's reasoning is correct. Summer says Mia will be a successful wildlife ranger **for sure** and Mia does appear to have the qualities needed. However, the information does not say that someone with those qualities will **definitely** be a successful wildlife ranger. Summer's reasoning is therefore flawed.

Jack's reasoning is also flawed. Jack tells us Alex is fit and interested in conservation but that he doesn't think Alex likes science. Since Jack does not know for sure that Alex is not interested in science, he cannot say being a wildlife ranger is **definitely** not for Alex.

33 In the first column, the two two-digit numbers must add to less than 200 (because the maximum two-digit number is 99). So K = 1.

In the third column, knowing that K = 1, the numbers must add to less than 300. So E = 2.

If K = 1 and E = 2, then from the first column P = 9. This means, from the first row, that L = 3.

Then, from the second column, as 3 + 3 = 6, H = 6. The statement that is not correct is Q = 6.

99	+	53	=	152
+		+		+
42	+	43	=	85
=		=		=
141	+	96	=	237

34 Questions like this are always easier to work out with a diagram. Something as simple as a line with arrows for trains can help you see the way to the answer.

The first train left at 3 pm and arrived at 6 pm so we can see it took the first train 3 hours to make the trip. If it was half as fast as the second train, the second train was twice as fast and must have completed the trip in half the time. So the second train completed the trip in 1 hour 30 minutes and arrived at 4:30 pm.

By dividing the trip into three parts we can see that when the first train has completed one part, the second train has completed two parts.

Looking at the diagram we can see that the trains pass after 1 hour, at 4 pm.

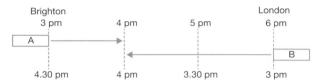

Brighton
3 pm   4 pm   5 pm   London
6 pm

A

B

4.30 pm   4 pm   3.30 pm   3 pm

35 If anyone who blew down the house must have been in the area yesterday and also must be very strong, then it follows that anyone who does not satisfy both requirements cannot have blown down the house. So if Mr Wolf was very weak rather than very strong, he cannot have blown down the house.

A and C are incorrect. Just because Mr Wolf did not blow down the house does not mean he cannot have been in the area yesterday or that he cannot be very strong.

D is incorrect. Just because Mr Wolf satisfies both requirements does not mean he **must** have blown down the house. There might also be others who satisfy both requirements. It only means Mr Wolf **might** have done it.

36 Once a tile is created it can only be rotated. It cannot be reflected. The pattern in C uses two types of tile, one a reflection of the other.

37 The code involves putting the person's name at the front of the alphabet so that A becomes the first letter of the name. B becomes the second letter, and so on, without repeating letters, and then following with the rest of the alphabet.

Using Graham's code we find out that the word is BREAD.

His friend has coded BREAD as EQAPY. This means B becomes E, R becomes Q, E becomes A, A becomes P and D becomes Y. So we can fill in some of the friend's code.

A	B	C	D	E	F	G	H	I	J	K	L	M
P	E		Y	A								
N	**O**	**P**	**Q**	**R**	**S**	**T**	**U**	**V**	**W**	**X**	**Y**	**Z**
				Q								

Considering the options we can see that the friend's name can only be Penny.

Here is the full code for her name:

A	B	C	D	E	F	G	H	I	J	K	L	M
P	E	N	Y	A	B	C	D	F	G	H	I	J
N	**O**	**P**	**Q**	**R**	**S**	**T**	**U**	**V**	**W**	**X**	**Y**	**Z**
K	L	M	O	Q	R	S	T	U	V	W	X	Z

38 Sanjay assumes that, since four films by students at his school won contests during the year, there were four students who created those films. However, it may be that some students won more than one film contest. In this case fewer than half of the qualifiers could be contest winners. So A shows the flaw in his reasoning.

The other options are incorrect. They are irrelevant and not mistakes Sanjay has made.

39 The manager claims that plantations with a single species of tree are good for the environment and play an important role in reducing carbon emissions because the trees store carbon. The statement that studies show single-species plantations emit more carbon than they absorb most weakens this claim since if the plantations emit more carbon than they store, they cannot be reducing carbon emissions.

A is incorrect. This statement weakens a general argument in support of plantation timber but doesn't **most** weaken the manager's claim.

B is incorrect. This statement might appear to support the manager's claim about the timber being a carbon store but actually refers to diverse forests, not single-species plantations. Without further information, such as D, it does not **most** weaken the manager's claim.

C is incorrect. This statement neither strengthens nor weakens the claim.

40 If four of the five dice are in sequence, the three possibilities are:

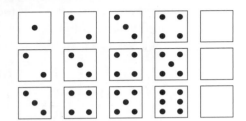

The total of the first possibility is $1 + 2 + 3 + 4 = 10$ so far. We cannot add another value to get 19 as there is no 9 on a normal dice. So rolling a 1 is not possible.

The total of the second possibility is $2 + 3 + 4 + 5 = 14$. The final dice is a 5 as $14 + 5 = 19$. So two fives are possible if a 2 is rolled.

The total of the third possibility is $3 + 4 + 5 + 6 = 18$. The final dice must be a 1 as $18 + 1 = 19$. So if Freya rolled a 6, she did not roll a 2 but she did roll a 1.

Option A is not true.

SAMPLE TEST 2

Page 14

1 A 2 D 3 D 4 B 5 B 6 C 7 D 8 B 9 A
10 B 11 C 12 D 13 A 14 C 15 A 16 D
17 B 18 C 19 C 20 C 21 A 22 A 23 C
24 B 25 B 26 C 27 A 28 D 29 A 30 D
31 A 32 D 33 D 34 C 35 A 36 C 37 D
38 C 39 C 40 C

1 There are six square tiles so each tile is made up of nine smaller squares.

The first tile shows the pattern. The centre square of each tile tells us how much it has been rotated. So the second tile across has been rotated 180° (half turn) and the tile beneath that is the first tile rotated 90° (quarter turn) in a clockwise direction.

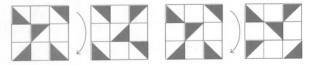

The missing part is the bottom three squares of the second tile and the top three squares of the tile beneath that one.

2 The conclusion is incorrect. Sally might have proven her ability and commitment but she still might not have won the scholarship. Proving commitment and ability only gives applicants a chance of winning the scholarship and does not guarantee they will achieve a scholarship for a place.

The other options are incorrect. These statements all show correct reasoning.

3 George is not 9, because that is Zac, or 10, because that is Oliver. He is not 11 because he sleeps in the bed next to the 11-year-old. He is not 12 because he has the green blanket and the 12-year-old has the brown blanket. So George is the 8-year-old.

The 12-year-old has the brown blanket so is not Isaac. He is not George, Zac or Oliver so he is Hiro. Isaac must be the 11-year-old. Now George sleeps between the 11-year-old and the bed with the red blanket. As Isaac has the bed on the far right, George must have the bed that is second from the right, meaning that the centre bed must have the red blanket.

4 Patrick needs to travel away and home again each day so will not use any one-way tickets. He wants to travel on Wednesday, Thursday and Friday of one week. The cost of three return tickets is $3 \times \$6$ or $18. So for the first week it is cheaper to buy a weekly ticket for $17. He should use the weekend pass, costing $5, for Saturday and Sunday. The cost of two return tickets for Monday and Tuesday of the second week is $2 \times \$6$ or $12.

The lowest price is $\$17 + \$5 + \$12$ or $34.

5 As $6 + 8 = 14$, the first column adds to 14 plus the unknown top-left number. The other two numbers in the diagonal which includes that same top number must also add to 14. As $5 + 9 = 14$, the number in the centre of the square must be 9.

As $6 + 9 = 15$, the other diagonal must add to 15 plus the unknown top-right number. The other two numbers in the last column must also add to 15. This means that the middle number of the last column must be 10.

Adding the numbers in the middle row, we have $8 + 9 + 10 = 27$. The total of all the rows, columns and diagonals must be 27.

13	2	12
8	9	10
6	16	5

6 To answer this question you must detect the flaw in Naseem's reasoning. You must work out something that Naseem has not thought of. The mistake or flaw in Naseem's reasoning is that he has not taken account of the fact that some students may have been a volunteer assistant coach on a minimum of eight occasions and also participated in four sporting activities themselves.

A and B are incorrect. These statements might be true but these issues are not mentioned by Nazeem in his comment so are not the mistake he has made.

D is incorrect. This is not the mistake shown by Naseem in his comment.

7 The circle and square indentations must be on different levels. This rules out C. The circle indentation is on a section of the piece that is a small rectangle. This rules out B. A and D are reflections of each other. The one that will fit with the original piece is D.

8 The argument is that time is running out to save the Great Barrier Reef from climate change. Option B adds additional information that strengthens the argument. It is further evidence about the importance of urgent action to save the reef.

A is incorrect. This is already stated in the text.

C is incorrect. This is about agricultural run-off, not the impacts of climate change.

D is incorrect. This is an explanation of how coral turns white, which is known as bleaching; it does not give additional evidence to strengthen the argument.

9 To answer this question you need to work out which sentence cannot be true in light of the information given. It cannot be true that competitors can win an Achievement Award even if they only come third in three out of three events because the information tells you

that competitors need to have competed in at least four events.

The other options are incorrect. These statements could all be true.

10 A cog that is enmeshed with another will turn by the same number of teeth. A cog that is attached by a belt to another one will turn at the same speed if the spindle around which the belt is wrapped is equal in diameter. So, in our case, the first two cogs will turn by the same number of teeth. The middle two cogs will make the same number of rotations. The final two cogs will turn by the same number of teeth.

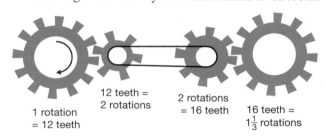

1 rotation = 12 teeth | 12 teeth = 2 rotations | 2 rotations = 16 teeth | 16 teeth = $1\frac{1}{3}$ rotations

11 You can conclude that open-pit mining radically changes landscapes because the information tells you that Ngwenya means crocodile in Swazi and the mountains were crocodile shaped before open-pit mining took place.

A is incorrect. This statement is probably true because it's likely that artifacts were found to enable the conclusion that the site is the oldest known mine in the world but the text does not tell you this.

B is incorrect. The text states this but there is no information in the text to support this conclusion.

D is incorrect. You cannot conclude that the San were more advanced technologically than the Bantu. You might, however, be able to conclude that the Bantu were more technologically advanced than the San because the Bantu people knew how to smelt iron.

12 To come to the conclusion that four entrants will get trophies, Katy has added the one trophy for People's Choice to the three trophies for first, second and third place. She has then assumed that the four trophies will go to four different students. She has not considered the possibility that the People's Choice winner might also come first, second or third—and therefore will receive two of the trophies, meaning only three students might get trophies.

A is incorrect. The information tells us each student can only enter one film. So this sentence shows a mistake, although it is not a mistake Katy has made.

B and C are incorrect. These statements might be true but they do not impact the number of trophies awarded and are not mistakes Katy has made.

13 *101 Dalmatians* can only be seen in Session 3. This means *Red Dog 2* must be seen in Session 2 and so *Red Dog* must be seen in Session 1 to make sure the movies are seen in the correct order. Charissa must choose her last movie from Session 4. *Milo and Otis* is not in Session 4 so cannot possibly be chosen.

14 The statement in C cannot be true. Rose finished second but was slower than Grace so Grace must have been first to finish the course.

A is incorrect. This statement could be true so it is not possible to state that it **cannot** be true.

B is incorrect. This statement is true.

D is incorrect. This statement could be true but, since we don't know how many obstacles Levi cleared, it is not possible to state that it **cannot** be true.

Name	Order finished	Obstacles cleared
Grace	1st	17
Ethan	3rd or 4th	19 or 20
George	5th	20
Rose	2nd	18
Levi	3rd or 4th	Not known

15 Wei's argument is that Anita can both study and go bushwalking because taking a break to go bushwalking will help her study. Research showing that spending time outdoors leads to better focus is further evidence to support the argument that the break outdoors will help Anita study.

B and C are incorrect. These statements are irrelevant to Wei's argument about the break helping Anita study.

D is incorrect. This statement might support an argument that Anita does not need to study. However, Wei's argument is that Anita can both study and go bushwalking so the statement is irrelevant to the argument.

16 Kirby visits the club three times per week. If the month is 28 days (exactly four weeks) she will visit the club only 12 times as 4 weeks × 3 visits = 12 visits. She visits the club 14 times so we need at least two more days in the month. But as the month starts on a Tuesday and Kirby does not visit the club on a Tuesday she will need more days. The month must have three more than 28 days. You can see from the calendar that the month must have 31 days.

Su	M	Tu	W	Th	F	Sa
30	31	1	2	3	4	5
6	7	8	9	10	11	12
13	14	15	16	17	18	19
20	21	22	23	24	25	26
27	28	29	30	31	1	2

17 The information tells us that everyone in favour of nachos was also in favour of fresh juices and no-one who was in favour of fresh juices was in favour of protein balls. So it is reasonable to draw the conclusion that if Norbit is in favour of nachos, he does not want protein balls.

A and C are incorrect. There is not enough information to draw these conclusions.

D is incorrect. The information tells us that everyone in favour of fresh juices was also in favour of a salad bar but it does not follow that everyone in favour of a salad bar was also in favour of fresh juices.

18 Both Nia's and Blake's reasoning is correct. Nia is correct because if their scores for performance were different but their scores for technical skills were the same, then their final exam scores could not be equal.

Blake is correct because if their scores for performance were the same but their scores for technical skills were different, then their final exam scores could not be equal.

19 As all those who like country also like classical, he cannot like country and pop without also liking classical. As he only likes three types of music, and one of them must be jazz, this is impossible.

20 Jayden shows correct reasoning because he recognises that Scarlet has a problem with nerves but feels that if she can overcome her nerves, she has a good chance of getting a prize so all her other recitation skills must be in place.

Conor shows correct reasoning because he recognises that Eden tends to overact but if she can tone down the acting and use appropriate dramatic presentation, he feels she could win a prize.

Both Jayden and Conor use low modality in presenting their opinions. Jayden says Scarlet has a **good chance**. Conor says Eden **could** win.

The other options are incorrect by a process of elimination.

21 If all the stools had just three legs, there would be a total of 3 × 18 legs. 3 × 18 = 6 × 9 = 54. There are an extra 61 – 54 or 7 legs. So seven stools must have had four legs.

22 To answer this question you need to evaluate each statement to determine whether or not the conclusion can be drawn from the information given. It cannot be true that containing urban sprawl will limit (control/restrict) the need for housing.

The other options are incorrect. They are all conclusions that can be drawn from the information in the box.

23 Total votes = 36 + 18 + 30 + 24 + 12 = 120. The graph has been divided into 20 parts. Now 120 ÷ 20 = 6. So each part represents 6 votes. Dividing each person's votes by 6 gives the number of parts on the graph each should have.

So Aziz should have 6 parts, Greg 3, Patricia 5, Theo 4 and Una 2. But the graph is divided into 4, 7, 3 and 6 parts. So the votes for Una must have been added to Patricia's votes.

24 Sanjeer's argument is that scooter laws vary from state to state in Australia and he'd like to see one set of rules for scooter use across the whole of Australia. B is the statement that most strengthens Sanjeer's argument.

A is incorrect. This could be a national e-scooter speed limit if there were national rules.

C is incorrect. This statement supports e-scooter speed limits but does not support Sanjeer's argument.

D is incorrect. This might be true but it does not support Sanjeer's argument in favour of one set of national laws.

25 Leo finished before Molly, who finished before Stella, who finished before Joseph. Abid finished last.

So Leo did finish first but Molly finished second, not third.

Abid got 10 questions correct and Molly got 8. Stella got more questions right than Joseph, who got more right than Leo. Remember that they all achieved different scores. Stella might have only got one question wrong and Joseph must have got at least 3 questions wrong.

26 The argument is that the British royal family is a colonial institution and therefore not deserving of people's admiration. The idea that a royal family is a good institution because it unites people and makes them proud of their nation weakens the argument that a royal family does not deserve its status, wealth or power.

A is incorrect. This statement supports Natalie's argument.

B is incorrect. This statement might be true but it is irrelevant to Natalie's argument.

D is incorrect. This statement might be true but it supports Natalie's argument because it presents a First Nations' perspective.

27 Sonia can only live in villa 1 or 2. Terry can only live in 1, 2 or 3. Wes can only live in 2, 3 or 4 and Dave can only live in 2 or 4. So Rachel lives in number 5.

If Dave lives in 2, then Sonia lives in 1, Terry lives in 3 and Wes lives in 4. The person with 1 child living 2 houses to the right of Terry would have to be Rachel, but then there would be no place for the villa with 4 children to the right of Wes. So Dave lives in number 4.

If Terry lives in 2, Sonia would have to live in 1. Then the villa that is 3 to the right of Sonia is number 4 and so is the villa that is 2 to the right of Terry, but they have different numbers of children. So Terry cannot live in number 2.

If Sonia lives in 1, Dave would live 3 to the right and would have 2 children. Terry would live in 3 and Rachel would have 1 child. Wes would live in 2, meaning that Sonia would have no children and Terry 4. Wes would have 3 children but 3 children live in an odd villa. So Sonia does not live in 1. She must live in number 2.

Terry cannot live in 3 if Sonia lives in 2 so Terry must live in number 1 and Wes must live in number 3. Rachel must have 2 children and Wes must have 1 child. The 3 children must live in number 1 and Wes is between 0 children in number 2 and 4 children in number 4. Sonia has no children.

	1	2	3	4	5	
left	Terry	Sonia	Wes	Dave	Rachel	right
	3	0	1	4	2	

28 It must be true that if Amelia did not have a motive, she cannot have been the one to pick the parsley.

A is incorrect. This statement is not logical. If opportunity and motive are required, and Amelia did not have an opportunity, then it does not make sense to state that she must have been the one to pick the parsley.

B is incorrect. This statement does not make sense because Amelia needed a motive to pick the parsley.

C is incorrect. This statement does not make sense because if Amelia picked the parsley, she would have needed an opportunity.

29 Alexander and George make contradictory statements. The bird cannot both be a magpie and not be a magpie. So either Alexander or George is the boy who is wrong. Frank and Steven must have both made correct statements, so the bird wasn't a peewee; it was a currawong. This means that George was correct; the bird wasn't a magpie. Alexander is the boy who was wrong.

30 The doctor claimed that the vaccination **always** prevented the disease. So, if the doctor is correct, a person who has been vaccinated will not have caught the disease. As Lisa caught the disease, if she has been vaccinated then the doctor is proved wrong. Max has been vaccinated, so if he caught the disease the doctor will be wrong. So, if either P or Q (or both) are Yes, the doctor is wrong. The only result that doesn't prove the doctor wrong is if both P and Q are No.

31 Since Max had regularly attended band rehearsals, the result of the teamwork challenge was not relevant in his case. Max only had to pass the music test in order to attend the music camp. Since he was not selected to attend, he must have failed the music test.

B is incorrect. This statement might be true. However, since Max had regularly attended band rehearsals, the result of the teamwork challenge was not relevant in his case. So it cannot be the reason he was not selected.

C is incorrect. The information tells us Max had regularly attended band rehearsals.

D is incorrect. Since Max had regularly attended band rehearsals, he only had to pass the music test to attend the music camp. So the statement that he did well in the test cannot be true since Max failed to be selected.

32 This statement is further evidence to support the argument that people should plant native gardens on their nature strips instead of grass that is time consuming to care for and still looks barren. Therefore this statement most strengthens the argument.

A is incorrect. This is a limitation when planting a native nature strip and could potentially weaken the argument.

B is incorrect. This is a restatement of a comment Ella has already made so it doesn't strengthen the argument.

C is incorrect. This statement is irrelevant to the argument so it does not strengthen it.

33 If 50 minutes on the pocket watch is equal to an hour, then 10 minutes on the pocket watch is equal to one-fifth of an hour, or 12 minutes.

Looking at the table we can see the relationship between Latika's watch and real time.

Latika's watch	Real time
10 minutes	12 minutes
20 minutes	24 minutes
30 minutes	36 minutes
40 minutes	48 minutes
50 minutes	60 minutes = 1 hour
60 minutes	**72 minutes**
70 minutes	84 minutes

Latika's pocket watch showed she had walked for 60 minutes. From the table we can see this is 72 minutes in real time, which is 1 hour and 12 minutes.

34 The 15 friends will need to hire a 28-seater bus for 4 days. The daily cost of that bus is $1200.

$$4 \times \$1200 = \$4800$$

so the friends will split $4800 evenly between the 15 of them.

$$\$4800 \div 15 = \$320$$

35 Zeynep is correct because if the Eastern Rockhopper is the only species of penguin that jumps feet first into the water then if you see a penguin jump feet first into the water, it must be an Eastern Rockhopper.

B is incorrect. Hugo's reasoning is not correct. The information tells us most penguins waddle. It also tells us that Eastern Rockhoppers are able to jump from one rock to another. So just because Eastern Rockhoppers are able to jump, it does not mean they never waddle.

C and D are incorrect by a process of elimination.

36 Once a tile is created it can only be rotated. It cannot be reflected. The only design that uses rotations only and has no reflections is C.

37 The square shape must be indented and the circle must protrude from the piece. This rules out B. The circle must be placed in the corner of the piece. This rules out A and C.

38 From the statements you can draw the conclusion that if Aisha is tired, then she will not do well in the test and will not stand a

chance of being offered a scholarship. So this conclusion is not possible.

A is incorrect. Even though Aisha stayed up late, she might not be tired. The statement says only that she'll likely be tired so she might do well in the test and still be offered the scholarship. Therefore this statement is possible.

B is incorrect. This statement is possible. The statement says that if Aisha does well in the test, she might be offered a scholarship—not that she'll definitely be offered one.

D is incorrect. This statement is possible.

39 Conner's statement would only be true if every student had a different name. If a student has the same name as another, you would only be able to find out which classes have a student with that name but you would not know which of these classes was correct. So this sentence shows the mistake he has made.

A is incorrect. The information in the box tells us the database can be used to look up any student so that must include new students.

B and D are incorrect. Neither of these statements are relevant and they are not mistakes Conner has made.

40 The 10 different paths are shown below.

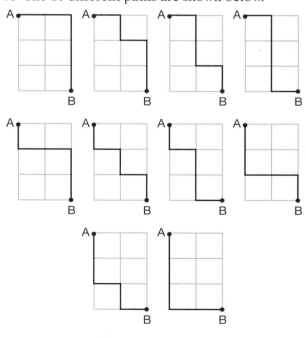

SAMPLE TEST 3

Page 24

1 B 2 A 3 C 4 C 5 B 6 C 7 D 8 B 9 A
10 A 11 C 12 B 13 B 14 B 15 C 16 A
17 A 18 D 19 D 20 B 21 C 22 C 23 B
24 D 25 B 26 A 27 A 28 C 29 D 30 D
31 D 32 C 33 D 34 B 35 C 36 D 37 C
38 B 39 A 40 A

1 Ben scored 10 goals and so did Jake. Lewis scored 2 fewer than Jake so Lewis scored 8 goals. Abdul scored 7 more goals than Lewis so Abdul scored 15 goals. Timothy scored more than 10 but less than 15.

The only correct option is that Abdul scored 15 goals.

2 Lei's argument is that Julia doesn't have to give up being a DJ to pursue a career as a full-time musician. The statement that any work in the music and entertainment industry supports a career as a musician strengthens Lei's argument.

B is incorrect. You are not told that Julia wants to earn more money.

C is incorrect. This argument is irrelevant to Julia's decision to focus on becoming a full-time musician.

D is incorrect. This statement weakens Lei's argument because practising to be a good DJ takes Julia's time away from pursuing her career as a musician.

3 The boy who came fifth wasn't Lachlan, Stathis, Xavier or Ehab so he was Thomas. Xavier finished after, but not immediately after, Ehab so Ehab must have finished second and Xavier fourth. Stathis must have come third and had the blue shirt. The boy in red finished after Xavier so Thomas had the red shirt. Ehab finished just before Stathis so had the green shirt and, as Stathis finished after the boy with the yellow shirt, Lachlan must have had the yellow shirt. Xavier had the remaining colour: white.

4 Derek has 6 more marbles than when the game started. So he must have spun an even number and both Hung and Matt must have spun odd numbers. For his spin, Derek would have received 2 marbles from Hung and 2 from Matt.

This would mean Derek had 29 marbles and Jordan and Matt both had 23. Hung would then have to give 1 marble to Derek and 1 to Matt, meaning that after Hung's spin Derek would have 30 marbles, Hung would have 21 and Matt would have 24. Finally, Matt would have to give a marble to Derek and one to Hung. So Derek would have 31, Hung would have 22 and Matt would have 22.

Alternatively if they each had 25 marbles to begin with, there must be a total of 75 marbles. If Derek had 31, then together Hung and Matt must have 44. As the result of all the spins must be the same for Hung and Matt, they must have the same number of marbles. $44 \div 2 = 22$.

5 The argument is that feral camels are a huge environmental problem for all the reasons listed. The information tells you there are hundreds of thousands of them in the wild. They eat native vegetation, trample sand dunes and their populations are difficult to manage. For these reasons you can conclude that camels must be well adapted to survive in very dry areas across Australia.

A and C are incorrect. These are ways of controlling camel populations and not conclusions you could draw from the text.

D is incorrect. This is already stated in the text and is not a conclusion you could draw from the text.

6 Samuel could pay $18 for the first 2 days and another $10 for the third. Similarly he could pay $18 for the 19th and 20th, and $10 for the 21st. He would pay $32 for the last 4 days.

$18 + $10 + $18 + $10 + $32 = $88

No other combination will produce a lower amount so the least amount that Samuel can pay is $88.

7 Neither Ava nor Fawad uses correct reasoning. Ava is incorrect because seahorses and sea dragons both live in Australian waters. She cannot conclude that the creature **must** be a seahorse. Fawad is incorrect. The information tells you sea dragons have longer snouts and tails than seahorses but, without another animal to compare it to, Fawad cannot tell if one creature on its own has a longer tail or snout.

The other options are incorrect by a process of elimination.

8 In the last square of the middle row, the top number must be 4 and the bottom number 1. The triangle on the left side of that square can only have 2 or 3 but, as the adjoining square already has a 2, the left side of the last square and the right side of the second-last square in the middle row must have 3.

In the second-last square of the bottom row, the right-side triangle will have 2. The top triangle cannot have 3 so it must have 4. So the left side has 3. The right side of the adjoining square (the middle one on the bottom row) must also have 3. This means that the shaded triangle cannot be 3.

The bottom triangle of the second-last square on the middle row must be 4. The remaining triangle in that square must be 1. The shaded triangle cannot be 1.

In the second square in the middle row, the top triangle must be 1. The left-side triangle cannot be 4 and the bottom triangle cannot be 4 (because 4 appears elsewhere in the adjoining squares). So that square must have 4 in the right-side triangle. The shaded triangle cannot be 4.

So the shaded triangle can only be 2.

9 It is not possible that Hamish prepared inadequately but was not dismissed from the team. The information provided states that inadequate preparation is severely frowned upon and debaters who are ill prepared will be dismissed.

B is incorrect. This is possible according to the rules. If Hamish did not have a good excuse for his absences, he would have been dismissed.

C is incorrect. This option is possible because you are told that positions on the debating team are highly prized and if a debater does not perform well or slips up in any way, they can lose their place on the team.

D is incorrect because it is possible that Hamish had a good excuse for not showing up for rehearsals and so was not dismissed.

10 B has the slanted section on the wrong side for it to fit. C similarly has the slanted section on the wrong side to fit and D is too wide to form a cube. A could fit to form a cube.

11 Sienna's mistake is that she has not realised the child who wins the cash prize for the highest scoring play might be a player who comes first, second or third. This would mean only three children would win cash prizes.

A is incorrect. This is not mentioned in the text so it is not the mistake Sienna has made.

B is incorrect. This is irrelevant to Sienna's mistake.

D is incorrect. This is not mentioned in the information about prizes.

12 Only Uma's reasoning is correct. She tells us Scamp has some of the qualities needed to be a **good** therapy dog but that his fear of thunder **might** be a problem with loud noises. Her reasoning is correct when she says Scamp **probably won't** make it as a therapy dog.

A is incorrect. Muffin appears to have the qualities needed to be a therapy dog. However, Luca's reasoning is flawed when he says Muffin would be a **great** therapy dog **for sure**.

C and D are incorrect by a process of elimination.

13 With 4 pulleys, Hafthor can lift up to 116 kg. By dividing by 4 we can find the amount he can lift without one.

$$116 \div 4 = 29 \text{ kg}$$

With 7 pulleys he can lift 7 times that amount.

$$29 \times 7 = 203 \text{ kg}$$

14 The physiotherapist's argument is that to be healthier, people need to do more than sit less—they need to move more and in a variety of positions. The fact that ballet dancers who perform repetitive positions suffer pain and health issues adds to this argument and strengthens it.

A is incorrect. This statement is irrelevant to the argument about moving more in a variety of ways.

C is incorrect. This statement summarises the physiotherapist's argument.

D is incorrect. This restates a comment already made by the physiotherapist and so does not add to the argument.

15 We know that any students who did not get a chance to be in the play last term **will** be given a chance to be in it this term. However, this does not mean that anyone who was in it last term will definitely **not** be given a chance to be in it again this term. Therefore this sentence shows the flaw in Kala's reasoning; she may still be able to be in the play this term.

A and B are incorrect. These sentences are true and are not mistakes made by Kala.

D is incorrect. This sentence is a mistake since the teacher said they definitely will be given a chance to perform this term. However, it is not a mistake made by Kala.

16 By looking at the departure and arrival times, we can see that it took Pete 42 minutes to walk to the restaurant and it took Kima 33 minutes. Kima will arrive home 33 minutes after they leave the restaurant. Pete will arrive home 42 minutes after they leave. 42 – 33 = 9 minutes. Kima arrives home 9 minutes earlier than Pete.

17 The mayor claims that the eco-friendly substitutes are of little value to ratepayers, yet 90% of ratepayers are in favour of eco-friendly substitutes. So this statement weakens the Mayor's claim.

B is incorrect. The mayor could use this statement to strengthen the claim.

C is incorrect. This statement could strengthen the claim.

D is incorrect. This statement neither strengthens nor weakens the claim.

18 If whoever won the athletic championship must have the athletic skill and also the ability to perform in competition conditions, then it follows that anyone who does not satisfy both requirements cannot have won the athletic championship. So, since Kale did not have the ability to perform in competition conditions, he cannot have won the championship.

A is incorrect. Just because Atiya did not win the championship, it does not mean she must not have had the ability to perform in competition conditions.

B is incorrect. Just because Breno satisfies both requirements, it does not mean that he must have won the championship. There might also be others who satisfied both requirements. It only means that Breno **might** have won it.

C is incorrect. Just because Stella did not win the championship, it does not mean she must not have athletic skill.

19 Looking at the blue lines at the edges of each of the missing pieces, they all have different numbers on the sides. Looking at the space marked *P*, there are no blue lines passing through the left-hand side. So the only possible option that can fit in space *P* is option D. It will need to be rotated 90° to the left to fit.

20 If Nicole stole the watch, then she would be lying and so would Kate, who says that Sarah stole the watch. This would mean two people are lying, which is not the case. In all other cases, it is possible for only one person to be lying while two people are telling the truth. For example, if none of the three stole the watch then Kate is lying when she says that Sarah stole it, but the other two are telling the truth when they say that they didn't steal it.

21 Option C cannot be true. The information tells us that every extra star on an appliance's rating is equal to a 20% reduction in its electricity consumption. This means a five-star appliance is superior in energy efficiency to a one-star appliance.

The other options are incorrect. These statements are true according to the information given.

22 Both Mehreen and Mitchell use correct reasoning. If the scores in two areas were the same, then the score in the third area must be the same to achieve equal scores.

The other options are incorrect by a process of elimination.

23 Alya is calling for donations to an Active Inclusion Sports Day for young people with disabilities. Her argument is that the event supports people with disabilities to be more active. The statement that increased activity promotes physical and mental health most strengthens Alya's argument.

A is incorrect. Although it shows the event has wide official and government support, it is not as supportive a statement of Alya's argument—to support people with disabilities to be more active for better health outcomes—as B.

C and D are incorrect. These statements only refer to aspects of mental health and don't mention physical health benefits. Therefore they are not as strongly supportive of Alya's argument as B.

24 Each small rectangle must be a mirror image of the ones it is next to, where the fold is the line of symmetry. The only option where this is the case is D.

25 The trip will cost $765 as it is for 6 people. This cost will then need to be divided between the five paying friends. $765 \div 5 = 153$. They will each pay $153.

26 The argument is that more electric wheelchairs should be made available at the shopping centre for those who want to use them. The fact that most people bring their own wheelchairs to the shopping centre weakens the argument that the centre should provide them.

B and C are incorrect. These statements strengthen the argument.

D is incorrect. This may be true but it is irrelevant to the argument that the centre should provide more electric wheelchairs for those who want to use them.

27 There were 9 children altogether. If they were all riding bicycles, there would be 9×2 or 18 wheels. As there are 20 wheels, that is 2 extra wheels so there must have been 2 tricycles. If there were 2 tricycles, there must have been $9 - 2$ or 7 bicycles.

28 Keira and Sophie made contradictory statements. The brother cannot both be 5 and not be 5 so one of those two were wrong. So Mary and Alana were both correct. Their brother is 4. Sophie is the sister who got it wrong.

29 The mistake River has made is not realising that sometimes there are streets with the same name across a number of suburbs. If he only enters a street name, the guidance system could take his family to the wrong suburb.

A is incorrect. This could be true but it is irrelevant to the mistake River has made.

B is incorrect. This is unlikely to be true in River's circumstance.

C is incorrect. This is not the mistake River has made.

30 If blue light in the day helps a person feel more alert, it is further evidence to support the argument that people should stay away from blue light at night if they want to fall asleep and stay asleep. Therefore D most strengthens that argument.

A is incorrect. This statement about red, orange and yellow light does not give any further evidence about blue light being bad for sleep so it neither strengthens nor weakens the argument.

B is incorrect. This statement provides a reason why getting sleep is important but it doesn't give any further evidence about blue light being bad for sleep. Therefore it neither strengthens nor weakens the argument.

C is incorrect. This statement neither strengthens nor weakens the argument.

31 If Jasmine's lotion works, then whenever the lotion is used the sting needs to be soothed. So, because Bill used the lotion, his sting needed to be soothed. The result P needs to be known.

If the sting has not been soothed, and Jasmine's lotion works, then Jasmine's lotion must not have been used. Freya's sting was not soothed so she needed to have not used the lotion. The result S needs to be known.

32 The information tells us everyone in favour of a family fun zone was also in favour of a DJ and no-one who was in favour of a DJ was in favour of face painting. So it is reasonable to draw the conclusion that if Finn is in favour of a family fun zone, he does not want face painting.

A is incorrect. The information tells us everyone who wants a family fun zone also wants a DJ.

B is incorrect. There is not enough information to draw this conclusion.

D is incorrect. The information tells us everyone who wants a DJ also wants roving performers but it does not follow that everyone who wants roving performers also wants a DJ.

33 Molly improves by 5 in both subjects. Her total improvement is 5 + 5 = 10 marks. Similarly Zach improves by 9 − 3 = 6, Otis improves by 0 + 9 = 9 and Lonnie improves by 3 + 8 = 11. Lonnie improves the most.

34 If it takes 16 minutes to drive the whole way, then it takes 4 minutes to go a quarter of the way, as 16 ÷ 4 = 4.

So when Becky drives three-quarters of the way she drives for 12 minutes then walks for 12 minutes to make a total trip time of 24 minutes.

It takes Becky 12 minutes to walk a quarter of the way so it will take 4 × 12 or 48 minutes to walk the whole way.

35 Both Lisa's and Jarrah's reasoning is correct. Lisa is correct because if their scores for the individual sequence were different but their scores for the fight match were the same, then their final exam scores could not be equal. Jarrah is correct because if their scores for the individual sequence were the same but their scores for the fight match were different, then their final exam scores could not be equal.

The other options are incorrect by a process of elimination.

36 If Tommy rolls a pair of 1s and a pair of 2s, he cannot total 16 as 1 + 1 + 2 + 2 = 6 and the fifth dice cannot show a 10.

If he rolls a pair of 4s and a pair of 5s, he also cannot total 16 as the sum of these four dice alone is 4 + 4 + 5 + 5 = 18. This also means he cannot roll a pair of 5s and a pair of 6s.

If Tommy rolls pairs on consecutive numbers, and the total of the dice is 16, he must roll one of the two options below.

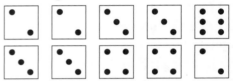

A is possible but isn't the answer that must be true. We can see above that he may roll a 2 without rolling a 6.

B is possible but isn't the answer that must be true. We can see above that he may roll a 3 without rolling a 4.

C is also possible.

However, the question asks what **must** be true.

We can see that if Tommy rolls a 4, he also rolls a single 2. The only answer that **must** be true is D.

37 Max found 5 boxes and Daniel found 4. Zoe found more boxes than Leo, who found more boxes than Niamh. So Zoe found 3 boxes, Leo 2 and Niamh 1.

Max found the least number of ribbons. Daniel found more ribbons than Niamh, who found more ribbons than Leo, who found more ribbons than Zoe. So Daniel must have found 5 ribbons, Niamh 4, Leo 3, Zoe 2 and Max 1.

The correct option, the one that cannot be true, is Leo did not find exactly three ribbons.

38 The restaurant owner claims that the beachfront restaurants have been able to increase their outdoor dining areas to allow more customers, yet a report to Council found no increase in customer numbers or spend for the beachfront businesses. So this statement weakens the restaurant owner's claim.

A is incorrect. This statement could strengthen a general argument in favour of extending the trial but it neither strengthens nor weakens the restaurant owner's argument about more customers.

C is incorrect. This statement neither strengthens nor weakens the restaurant owner's argument about more customers.

D is incorrect. This statement that there were divided views about the street closure neither strengthens nor weakens the argument.

39 Zara has assumed that since three state skateboarding records were broken, there were three qualifiers who broke those records. However, it may be that a qualifier broke more than one record. In this case fewer than half of the qualifiers could be record-breakers. So A shows the flaw in Zara's reasoning.

The other options are incorrect. These statements are irrelevant and are not mistakes Zara has made.

40 Huan is drinking a milkshake and Darcy is drinking orange juice so the boy who is drinking water must be Oliver. The girls must be the ones drinking lime cordial, cola and lemonade.

Anna and Sara are sitting next to each other and so are Oliver and Fatima. These pairs must be sitting on opposite sides of the table. Either Oliver or Fatima must be the person in the centre of their side and that person is opposite Anna and drinking lime cordial. She must be Fatima.

The person drinking cola is sitting opposite Darcy. She is not Anna or Fatima so must be Sara.

Anna must be the person drinking lemonade.

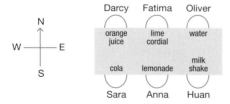

	Darcy	Fatima	Oliver
	orange juice	lime cordial	water
			milk shake
	cola	lemonade	
	Sara	Anna	Huan

SAMPLE TEST 4   Page 35

1 D 2 A 3 A 4 B 5 A 6 B 7 C 8 D 9 C
10 C 11 C 12 D 13 C 14 B 15 A 16 A
17 D 18 C 19 D 20 B 21 B 22 A 23 D
24 C 25 D 26 D 27 C 28 A 29 B 30 C
31 A 32 A 33 C 34 C 35 B 36 B 37 C
38 D 39 C 40 A

1 Mo, Nathan and Ali each collected more than 19 and less than 32 stickers. Mo collected 6 more than Nathan but 4 less than Ali. So either Nathan has 20, Mo 26 and Ali 30 or Nathan has 21, Mo 27 and Ali 31. In either case Ali has 10 more stickers than Nathan. The other options might be correct but the one that must be correct is D.

2 Scarlet uses low modality to suggest she thinks that if Yoshiyaki develops confidence, he'll be successful as a magician. Her reasoning allows for Yoshiyaki's weakness.

B is incorrect. Leo cannot assert that he's sure Isobel will be a successful magician. He knows she doesn't practise enough and makes mistakes. Practice is essential according to the information in the box so if Scarlet won't practise, she cannot become successful. Leo is incorrect.

The other answers are incorrect by a process of elimination.

3 The person from Tennyson is not Mimi, Jye or Phoebe. That person cannot be Troy. So Noah must be the person who lives in Tennyson.

The person who lives in Jerseyville is not Troy and cannot be Jye. Neither Noah nor Phoebe live in Jerseyville so the person who does must be Mimi.

Because Mimi lives in Jerseyville, Jye does not live in Milton (no two people have the same pair of initials). Jye does not live in Jerseyville, Milton, Norwood or Tennyson. He can only live in Palmyra.

4 The fact that other units all have white blinds weakens Jasmine's application.

The other options are incorrect. These statements are all supportive of Jasmine's argument. Jasmine has applied for a black blind which complies with the building's by-laws (A); the fact that the blinds will reduce electricity costs and reduce the impact on the planet is strongly supportive of Jasmine's application (C); and acknowledging that the blind will comply with building codes, safety standards and the building's by-laws also strongly supports Jasmine's argument (D).

5 Find the cost for each choice.

2 boxes of 8 and 1 single cake cost
$2 \times \$12 + \$2$ or $26.

1 box of 8 and 3 packets of 3 cost
$\$12 + 3 \times \$5$ or $27.

5 packets of 3 and 2 single cakes cost
$5 \times \$5 + 2 \times \$2$ or $29.

17 single cakes cost $17 \times \$2$ or $34.

The best price is $26 when 2 boxes of 8 and a single cake are bought.

6 If the key belongs to William, then his statement 'This is not my key' is false. Then, because at least one of his statements must be true, his second statement 'It is Oscar's key' must be true. But if the key belongs to William, it cannot also belong to Oscar. So the key does not belong to William.

7 Because Aiden had proof of his songwriting ability he only needed to pass the interview. He must have done badly in the interview to have failed to be accepted for the workshops.

A is incorrect. Aiden did not have to pass the songwriting challenge because he had proof of his songwriting ability.

B is incorrect. If Aiden had done well in the interview, he would have been accepted for the workshops.

D is incorrect. Aiden had proof of his songwriting ability.

8 The argument calls for the protection of forests and cites a number of reasons for doing so. The statement that tropical forests contain more than half of all the world's plant and animal species adds further support to the argument.

A is incorrect. This is already stated in the argument to protect forests.

B is incorrect. This statement might be true but it is not a significant reason to save the world's forests.

C is incorrect. This statement might be true but the argument that many people depend on forests for their livelihoods is already included in the text.

9 If Logan lost round 1 only, he would have
$25 - 1 + 2 + 4 + 8 = 38 \neq 32$.

If Logan lost round 2 only, he would have
$25 + 1 - 2 + 4 + 8 = 36 \neq 32$.

If Logan lost round 3 only, he would have
$25 + 1 + 2 - 4 + 8 = 32$.

If Logan lost round 4 only, he would have
$25 + 1 + 2 + 4 - 8 = 24 \neq 32$.

Jennifer won Round 3.

10 If Kimberley is exactly halfway between Cape Town and Pretoria, and the train stops for 1 hour there, it must take 15 hours to go from Kimberley to either Cape Town or Pretoria.

Cape Town	15 hrs	1 hr stop Kimberley	15 hrs	= 31 hrs Pretoria

How many hours after 9am Tuesday will the train arrive at Kimberley? We must add all the hours together, including the full one-way trip, the stopover and the return to Kimberley.

$31 + 18 + 15 = 64$ h $= 2 \times 24 + 16 = 2$ days 16 h

2 days and 16 hours after 9 am Tuesday is 1 am Friday.

11 Owen uses correct reasoning when he says he doesn't think professional photography will suit Frankie due to her lack of organisation and poor attention to detail.

Halyna uses correct reasoning to declare that Adam is likely to make a great professional photographer. She uses the low-modality term 'is likely' rather than the high-modality term 'will' so although she seems confident of his abilities, she still allows room for the possibility that he will not become a great professional photographer.

The other options are incorrect by a process of elimination.

12 Option D cannot be true. Eli finished second but was slower than Aziz so Aziz must have been first to finish the quiz.

A is incorrect. This statement could be true so it isn't possible to say it **cannot** be true.

B is incorrect. This statement is true.

C is incorrect. This statement could be true since we do not know how many quiz questions Lucia got correct. So it isn't possible to say it **cannot** be true.

Making a table can be helpful.

Name	Order finished	Quiz questions correct
Aziz	1st	17
Ying	3rd or 4th	19 or 20
Marina	5th	20
Eli	2nd	18
Lucia	3rd or 4th	Not known

13 The result of the multiplication is 18. The options for the two numbers are: 1 and 18, 2 and 9, or 3 and 6. A shift of 1 together with a shift of 18 is a total shift of 19. A shift of 2 together with one of 9 is a total shift of 11. Shifts of 3 and 6 mean a total shift of 9.

	A	B	C	D	E	F	G	H	I	J	K	L	M
19	T	U	V	W	X	Y	Z	(A)	B	C	D	E	F
11	L	M	N	O	P	Q	R	S	T	U	V	W	X
9	J	K	L	M	N	O	P	Q	R	S	T	U	V

	N	O	P	Q	R	S	T	U	V	W	X	Y	Z
19	G	H	I	J	K	L	M	N	O	P	Q	R	S
11	Y	Z	(A)	B	C	D	E	F	G	H	I	J	K
9	W	X	Y	Z	(A)	B	C	D	E	F	G	H	I

A shift of 19 means that A would be written for an H.

A shift of 11 means that A would be written for a P.

A shift of 9 means that A would be written for an R.

This means S is the option that is not possible.

14 Amanda's statement would only be true if every street name was unique. If some streets have the same name as each other, you would only be able to find out which suburbs had a street of that name—not the exact suburb of the specific street you are looking for.

A is incorrect. The information tells us the directory is up-to-date and this statement is not a mistake Amanda has made.

C is incorrect. Even if this statement is true, it is not a mistake Amanda has made.

D is incorrect. You would still be able to look up those streets and find this out so it is not a mistake Amanda has made.

15 The BVA argument is that volleyball is increasing in popularity and so needs extra court space. The fact that players need to set up extra impromptu 'courts' supports this argument that there is currently not enough space. Also the statement that it is the messy nature of these impromptu courts that other beach users do not like, rather than the extra space they take up, could also support the BVA argument.

B is incorrect. This statement is irrelevant to the BVA argument that volleyball is increasing in popularity and so needs extra court space.

C is incorrect. This statement would weaken the BVA's argument for more court space

D is incorrect. The BVA has already mentioned this in their argument. This statement does not add anything further to strengthen that argument.

16 As the teeth of cogs mesh, the two cogs turn in opposite directions. The below diagram shows the turning direction of each cog. We can see that the weights 1 and 4 will go up, meaning the weights 2 and 3 will go down.

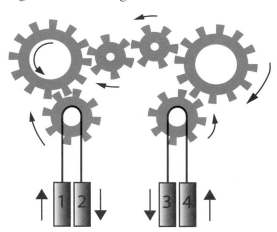

17 Neither Chloe's nor Malik's reasoning is correct. Chloe's reasoning that the motor temperature must be okay since the light isn't flashing is flawed. The manual says that the light flashing means the motor is about to overheat but that does not rule out the possibility that the motor could overheat without the light flashing. Malik's reasoning that the continuous red light must mean the motor has already overheated is also flawed. There is no information given about the meaning of a continuous light and the meaning of a continuous light does not necessarily follow from the meaning of a flashing light.

The other options are incorrect by a process of elimination.

18 The information tells us that everyone in favour of a police officer was also in favour of a filmmaker and no-one who was in favour of a filmmaker was in favour of a politician. So it is reasonable to draw the conclusion that if Poppy is in favour of a police officer, she also wants a filmmaker and so does not want a politician.

A is incorrect. The information tells us that everyone who wants a police officer also wants a filmmaker.

B is incorrect. There is not enough information to draw this conclusion.

D is incorrect. The information tells us that everyone who wants a filmmaker also wants a journalist but it does not follow that everyone who wants a journalist also wants a filmmaker.

19 The sum of the sides of opposite sides must be 11. The triangle (3 sides) must be opposite the octagon (8). The square (4) must be opposite the heptagon (7) and the pentagon (5) must be opposite the hexagon (6). When D is folded, the square is opposite the hexagon. The sum of the sides of those two shapes is 10. The octagon is opposite the triangle. The sum of the sides of those shapes is 11. The pentagon and heptagon (with a sum of 12 sides) are opposite each other.

20 Daisy uses correct reasoning to declare that a seahorse giving birth to young sea horses can't be a female.

A is incorrect. Asif uses incorrect reasoning to declare that any seahorse laying eggs must be a male. The information tells you that male seahorses carry eggs but not that they lay them.

The other options are incorrect by a process of elimination.

21 It is not possible that Luca was allowed to watch the episode live if he didn't get his homework done by 7 pm.

The other options are incorrect. These statements are all possible.

22 The only people we know who like dogs are those who like rabbits and those who like horses. Similarly the only people we know of who like cats are those who like rabbits and those who only like cats. But the third statement tells us that there are more people who like cats than those who like horses. Therefore there are more people who like cats than like horses and rabbits combined.

The other options are all possible but not necessarily true.

23 The information does not say that if you had a speaking part last term, you will not get one this term. Zihao is mistaken. He could be given a speaking part again this term.

The other options are incorrect. These are not mistakes Zihao has made.

24 Lani completes 12 laps in 10 minutes. That is four lots of 3 laps ($4 \times 3 = 12$). In the same time, Holly will have completed four lots of 2 laps, which is 8 laps ($4 \times 2 = 8$). If it takes Holly 10 minutes to ride 8 laps, it takes 5 minutes to ride 4 laps. She needs to ride 4 more laps to complete the race, which will take an extra 5 minutes. Lani will beat her by 5 minutes.

25 The darkest spot must be adjacent to the second darkest spot as they will be touching when the paper is folded. The second darkest spot must also be adjacent to the third darkest spot for the same reason. The lightest spot must be adjacent to the third darkest spot for the same reason and will go in the remaining section of the paper. This rules out B and C. Also each image must be the mirror image of those adjacent. This rules out A. The correct solution is D.

26 Five houses have 3 dogs and 11 have 2.

$5 \times 3 = 15$ and $11 \times 2 = 22$. As $15 + 22 = 37$, this accounts for 37 dogs altogether.

As $53 - 37 = 16$, there are another 16 dogs and these must all live in houses that have just one dog. $5 + 11 + 16 = 32$ so 32 houses have dogs. $45 - 32 = 13$ so the remaining 13 houses do not have a dog.

27 C is the only option that **must** be true. The other options **could** be true. From the information given, anyone who likes art likes drama and (since they like drama) they also like dance but not choir. It is therefore not possible for someone who likes art to like choir so C must be true.

The other options are incorrect. These options could be true.

A is incorrect. The information tells you that everyone who likes drama likes dance but not that everyone who likes dance likes drama.

B is incorrect. The information does not tell you whether people who do not like choir also do not like dance. It only tells you that people who like drama do not like choir.

D is incorrect. You are told that everyone who likes art also likes drama. You are not told that if you don't like art, you don't like drama.

28 Option A provides additional support to strengthen the main argument that hula dancing is a complex cultural and spiritual dance where every tiny movement carries meaning.

B is incorrect. This is already stated in the text so does not strengthen the argument.

C is incorrect. This is interesting information about the history of hula dancing but it does not strengthen the argument.

D is incorrect. The fact that dancers train for years attests to the fact that hula dancing is complex. However, this is not the statement that most strengthens the argument that hula dancing is a complex cultural and spiritual dance.

29 Suppose both statements on the red box are false. This would mean that the first statement on the green box is true. But, if that is true, then the second statement on the red box would also be true. So both statements on the red box cannot be false.

The first statement on the green box is false. The second statement on the blue box cannot then be true. So both the blue and green boxes have at least one false statement. The red box must be the box that has two true statements.

This means the prize is in the blue box so the first statement on the blue box is also false. The blue box is the box with two false statements so the green box is the box with one true and one false statement. The first statement on the green box is false so the second one must be true. It is a cash prize.

30 The argument is that it is becoming more acceptable to throw away a broken item and buy a new one, with the supporting evidence that it is cheaper to replace it than get it fixed. The statement that Repair Cafes have skilled volunteers who repair items for free most weakens the claim because it takes away the supporting evidence.

A is incorrect. This is already mentioned in the supporting evidence for the claim so cannot weaken it.

B is incorrect. This statement could weaken the claim if it only mentioned the growing waste crisis as a consequence of throwing out rather than repairing items. However, the statement says that people like these cheap goods regardless of the consequences so it strengthens rather than weakens the claim.

D is incorrect. This statement supports the claim.

31 The graph doesn't tell us what each division on the vertical axis represents but we can still compare the amounts of each. White cars can easily be found on the graph because that is the most. It is the last bar. The number of white cars is equal to the number of red cars plus the number of black cars, so the only possible pairing of red and black cars is the third and fourth bars. There are half as many black as silver cars so black must be the fourth bar. Red is the third bar and silver the second bar, meaning that blue must be the first bar.

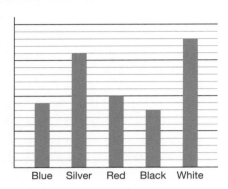

Now consider each option.

The statement in A is not true. There are more silver cars than red cars.

The statement in B is true. The fewest number is black cars.

The statement in C is true. There are twice as many white cars as blue cars.

The statement in D is true. Silver plus white is 16 + 18 = 34 divisions. Blue plus black is 9 + 8 = 17 divisions and 34 = 2 × 17.

The statement that is not correct is the statement in option A.

32 Since Oliver had previously volunteered to mentor younger students, the result of the debating challenge was not relevant in his case. Oliver only had to pass the teamwork assessment to be selected. Since he was not selected to attend, he must have failed the teamwork assessment.

B is incorrect. This statement might be true. However, since Oliver had previously volunteered to mentor younger students, the result of the debating challenge was not relevant in his case. So it cannot be the reason he was not selected.

C is incorrect. The information tells us that Oliver had previously volunteered to mentor younger students in the school.

D is incorrect. Since Oliver had previously volunteered to mentor younger students, he only had to pass the teamwork assessment to be selected. So this statement that he did well in the assessment cannot be true since Oliver failed to be selected.

33 Of those who improved their ranking, Eden went from equal 2nd to 1st, Romelu went from 5th to 4th, Robin went from 7th to 5th and Lucas went from 8th to 7th. Robin improved his rank among his teammates by two positions, whereas the other players only improved by one.

34 The three possible options for the order of the balls are shown below (it doesn't matter which ball starts on the left as the balls travel in a circuit).

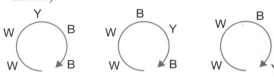

We can see that a black ball is always either in front of or behind a white ball.

35 We know that any Year 6 students who did not get a chance to attend the Youth Voices Forum last year **will** be given a chance to attend this year. However, this does not mean that anyone who attended last year will definitely **not** be given a chance to attend again this year. So this sentence shows the flaw in Santi's reasoning and he may still be able to attend this year.

A and C are incorrect. These sentences are true and are not mistakes Santi has made.

D is incorrect. This sentence is a mistake, since the principal said they **will definitely** be given a chance to attend this year, but it is not a mistake Santi has made.

36 If the shapes are numbered from 1 to 6, they move according to the same pattern across the steps: 1 goes to 6, 2 to 4, 3 to 5, 4 to 3, 5 to 1 and 6 to 2.

37 The pony club and sea scouts received the same amount and the sea scouts received $5000 so the pony club must have also received $5000. The cricket club received $2000 less than the pony club so the cricket club received $3000. The men's shed received $6000 more than the cricket club so the men's shed received $9000, which is $4000 more than the sea scouts. The tennis club received more than the pony club but less than the men's shed so it received between $5000 and $9000. The only statement that must be true is that all the grants were less than $10000.

38 Tim's father mentions that insects are gaining attention as a sustainable source of protein for people but his argument is also that insects can provide nutrition for plants. D provides evidence to support this claim so it is the one that most strengthens it.

A is incorrect. This provides more information about insects as food for people, not about nutrition for plants.

B is incorrect. This provides information about the sustainability of insect farming versus meat farming but Tim's father's argument is about the nutritional benefit of insects for plants.

C is incorrect. This statement is irrelevant to the argument so it does not strengthen it.

39 Xavier is correct because if the three-spined toadfish is the only species of fish that cries like a baby, then any fish that cries like a baby must be a three-spined toadfish. For the same reason if an animal that cries like a baby is not a three-spined toadfish, then it cannot be a fish. So Melia's reasoning is also correct.

The other options are incorrect by a process of elimination.

40 Milly's office number is higher than Luke's and Fahad's office is between them. So Milly's office number is higher than both Luke's and Fahad's. Her office number is lower than Aaron's, which is lower than Beth's. So the order, from 1 to 5, must be Luke, Fahad, Milly, Aaron, Beth.

Milly has office 3.

SAMPLE TEST 5

Page 45

1 C 2 C 3 D 4 B 5 A 6 A 7 D 8 B 9 D
10 C 11 B 12 D 13 B 14 B 15 A 16 A
17 C 18 C 19 A 20 D 21 C 22 B 23 A
24 D 25 C 26 B 27 D 28 D 29 B 30 B
31 D 32 B 33 C 34 B 35 B 36 C 37 A
38 A 39 A 40 D

1 Darcy is older than Bonnie, but the sum of the ages of Bonnie and Hannah is twice that of Darcy. Hannah must be older than Darcy (and Bonnie). Hannah is also older than Leonie and Jeremy. Hannah is either 10 or 12. But if Hannah is 12, there is no possible age for Bonnie and Darcy that would mean that the sum of the ages of Bonnie and Hannah was twice that of Darcy. So Hannah must be 10. Bonnie must be 4 and Darcy 7.

Both Leonie and Jeremy are younger than Hannah so Tyson must be the child who is 12. Leonie is older than Jeremy so Jeremy must be 5 and Leonie 9.

The child who is 9 years old is Leonie.

2 Charlotte and Austin both use flawed reasoning. The information stresses that battery buttons are dangerous but tempting items for small children and advises you to keep them, and items with button batteries in them, away from small children.

Charlotte states that her sister tries to open devices that have button batteries in them. It could only be a matter of time before the sister manages to open a device and get to the battery. Austin says his little brother enjoys a game of trying to get to the air-conditioning remote control faster than anyone else. It may only be a matter of time before his brother manages to get to a battery.

The other options are incorrect by a process of elimination.

3 Jacob can make all four of them.

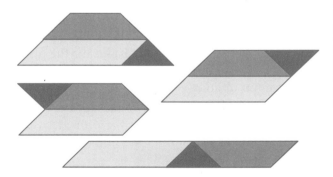

4 The car is faster than the truck so it will arrive before the truck. The truck travels for 4 h.

For every 3 h the truck travels, the car travels for 2 h. If we divide these values by 3, we can find out how long the car travels for every hour the truck travels.

2 h = 2 × 60 min = 120 min and 120 min ÷ 3 = 40 min.

This means that for every 1 h the truck travels, the car travels for 40 min. So if the truck travels for 4 h to complete a journey, the car will travel for 4 × 40 = 160 min = 2 h 40 min to complete the same journey. The car will arrive 2 h 40 min after 7 am at 9:40 am.

5 They each begin with 25 marbles. Jo must give each player 2 marbles at the result of her first spin, so Jo will have 21 marbles and Felix and Meg will both have 27. Felix will receive 3 marbles from the other players at the result of his first spin, so Jo will have 18 marbles, Felix will have 33 and Meg will have 24.

In the second round, after Jo's spin Jo will have 24, Felix 30 and Meg 21 marbles. After Felix's spin, Jo will have 23 marbles, Felix 32 and Meg 20. At the end of the second round, both Jo and Felix have 4 more marbles, so Meg must have spun 4 and given 4 marbles to each of them.

6 The argument is that people who are hearing impaired should have an alerting device to alert them if the smoke alarm goes off. Thus the statement that bed shakers are especially invaluable for hearing impaired people who live alone most strengthens that argument.

The other options are incorrect. These statements do not strengthen the argument.

7 From Gaynor, Nigel can buy 3 pies for the price of 2. So he can buy 3 pies for 2 × $5.50 or $11. He can buy 12 pies for 4 × $11 or $44.

From Sandra, Nigel can buy 4 pies for the price of 3. So he can buy 4 pies for 3 × $5 or $15. He can buy 12 pies for 3 × $15 or $45.

From Holly, Nigel can buy 2 pies for 2 × $4.40 or $8.80. He can then buy a third pie for half of $4.40 or $2.20. This means that 3 pies cost $8.80 + $2.20 or $11 and 12 pies cost 4 × $11 or $44.

From Joanne, Nigel can buy 3 pies for 3 × $4 or $12. He can then buy a fourth pie for half of $4 or $2. This means that 4 pies cost $12 + $2 or $14 and 12 pies cost 3 × $14 or $42.

The least amount Nigel can pay for 12 pies is $42 if he buys from Joanne.

8 If he was not born in England, then the second part of both the first and third statements would have to be true. However, the teacher cannot have both lived in Australia since he was five and moved to Australia when he was seven. The statement that he was born in England must be true. (The true part of the second statement must be that he wasn't born in New Zealand. He might or might not have lived in Australia since he was five, or moved to Australia when he was seven.)

9 Just because Louis has talent and time to rehearse, it does not mean that he must be chosen as lead actor—only that he **could** be chosen.

The other options are incorrect. All of these sentences could be true.

10 Option C must be true. From the information given, anyone who supports computer lessons supports learning Japanese and (since they support Japanese) they also support learning a musical instrument but not the Chess Club. It is therefore not possible for someone who supports computer lessons to also support the Chess Club.

11 Josh argues that, ahead of her exam, Melani should listen to music that plays at 60 beats per minute because that is the best tempo to encourage alpha brainwaves. If alpha brainwaves signal a calm and focused mind, this would be a good mental state to be in for an exam. So this statement supports and most strengthens Josh's argument.

A is incorrect. This statement might be true and could support an argument from Melani about listening to music before the exam but it does not strengthen Josh's argument.

C is incorrect. This statement is irrelevant to Josh's argument that Melani should add music that plays at 60 beats per minute to her playlist because that is the best tempo to encourage alpha brainwaves.

D is incorrect. This statement could be used to support Josh's argument; however, the more specific statement about the benefits of alpha brainwaves (B) **most** strengthens his argument.

12 If whoever was elected Patrol Leader must have been both approved by the Scoutmaster and ranked Second Class or higher, then it follows that anyone who does not satisfy both requirements cannot have been elected Patrol Leader. So, since Ruby was not ranked Second Class or higher, she cannot have been elected Patrol Leader.

A is incorrect. Just because Oscar was not elected Patrol Leader, it does not mean that he must not have been ranked Second Class or higher.

B is incorrect. Just because Talia satisfies both requirements, it does not mean that she must have been elected Patrol Leader. There might have been others who satisfied both requirements so it only means that Talia **might** have been elected.

C is incorrect. Just because Locky was not elected Patrol Leader, it does not mean that he was not approved by the Scoutmaster.

13 The cipher involves reversing the order of the alphabet so A becomes Z and B becomes Y. If Heather treats each 13-letter block separately, she will do this twice with A becoming M and N becoming Z. The cipher is shown below. Notice that the middle letter of each section (G and T) does not change.

A	B	C	D	E	F	G	H	I	J	K	L	M
M	L	K	J	I	H	G	F	E	D	C	B	A
N	O	P	Q	R	S	T	U	V	W	X	Y	Z
Z	Y	X	W	V	U	T	S	R	Q	P	O	N

The correct way for her to write GREAT is GVIMT.

14 Only Sophie's reasoning is correct. She tells us that Harry loves insects and is good at observing them but that he does not **seem** comfortable handling them. Her reasoning is correct when she says that Harry **probably** wouldn't be a successful entomologist. He may, in fact, be comfortable handling insects. Or he may become comfortable handling them. So Sophie is correct not to say that he **definitely** wouldn't be a successful entomologist.

A is incorrect. Luna appears to have the qualities needed to be a successful entomologist. However, Faisal's reasoning is flawed when he says that Luna would be a successful entomologist **for sure**.

The other options are incorrect by a process of elimination.

15 Tim Smith claims that Deep Creek Reserve has a long history and is well known by that name, yet it was only named five years ago. So this statement weakens his argument.

B and C are incorrect. These statements neither strengthen nor weaken the argument about Deep Creek Reserve having a long history.

D is incorrect. This statement could strengthen Tim Smith's argument rather than weaken it.

16 David assumes that since four poetry competitions were won, there were four qualifiers who won those competitions. However, it may be that a qualifier won more than one competition. In this case it would not be true that more than half of David's school's qualifiers were competition winners. So A shows the flaw in David's reasoning.

The other options are incorrect. These sentences are irrelevant and are not mistakes David has made.

17 As the teeth of the cogs mesh, the two cogs turn in opposite directions. If two cogs are connected by a belt instead of by meshing, the cogs will turn in the same direction. The following diagram shows the turning direction of each cog. We can see that weights 2 and 3 will go up, meaning that weights 1 and 4 will go down.

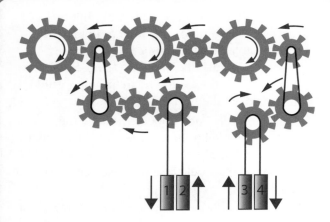

18 From the information given you can draw the conclusion that if Dora was not prepared, there is no way she will be offered a place in the Zone team. So this conclusion cannot be true.

A is incorrect. This statement might be true. Even though Dora did not go to training, she might still be prepared and so may play well and be offered a place in the Zone team.

B is incorrect. This statement might be true. Dora might have gone to training but still not have been offered a place in the Zone team.

D is incorrect. This statement might be true. The information tells us that if all the conditions are met, Dora **might** be offered a place in the Zone team—not that she will **definitely** be offered a place.

19 When folded, the triangle (3 sides) will be opposite the octagon (8). The square (4) will be opposite the heptagon (7) and the pentagon (5) will be opposite the hexagon (6).

If a triangle or octagon is rolled, the score is $3 \times 8 = 24$.

If a square or heptagon is rolled, the score is $4 \times 7 = 28$.

If a pentagon or hexagon is rolled, the score is $5 \times 6 = 30$.

The difference between the minimum and maximum scores is $30 - 24 = 6$.

20 The information tells us that everyone in favour of Tune Room was also in favour of Mozart Room and that no-one who was in favour of Mozart Room was in favour of Rap Room. So it is reasonable to draw the conclusion that if Ilkay is in favour of Tune Room, he also likes

Mozart Room and therefore does not like Rap Room.

A is incorrect. The information tells us that everyone who liked Tune Room also liked Mozart Room.

B is incorrect. There is not enough information to draw this conclusion.

C is incorrect. The information tells us that everyone who liked Mozart Room also liked Music Room, but it does not follow that everyone who likes Music Room also likes Mozart Room.

21 Option C cannot be true. Since group three was the second fastest to build its bridge and group three was not as fast as group one, it must be that group one was the fastest. Therefore group one was the first group to finish building its raft.

A is incorrect. This sentence might be true but, as we do not have enough information, it is not possible to state that it **cannot** be true.

B is incorrect. This sentence is true.

D is incorrect. Since we do not know how many cars group five's bridge held, we do not have enough information to say whose bridge collapsed with the fewest cars. Therefore it is not possible to state that this statement **cannot** be true.

Making a table can help.

	Speed to build	**Number of cars**
Group one	1st	2
Group two	5th	5
Group three	2nd	3
Group four	3rd or 4th	4 or more
Group five	3rd or 4th	No information

22 All those who like Supreme also like Hawaiian. So, if Colin likes Supreme and Vegetarian, he must also like Hawaiian.

23 Evie's argument is that Isaac will still have time to sleep and that taking a break to attend the painting workshop will help him relax and not feel stressed. The statement that research shows creative activities reduce stress levels supports and strengthens this argument.

B and C are incorrect. These statements might be reasons to attend the workshop but they do not strengthen the argument about the workshop helping Isaac to relax and not be so stressed.

D is incorrect. This statement is irrelevant to Evie's argument about the workshop helping Isaac to relax and not be so stressed.

24 If the first digit is 4, so is the sixth digit. The last two digits of the code form a two-digit number, so the fifth digit is not 0. If the fifth digit is 3 lots of the second, it must be 3, 6 or 9, and the second digit must be 1, 2 or 3. The possible codes are:

4 1 – – 3 4   or   4 2 – – 6 4   or   4 3 – – 9 4.

The middle two digits must form a two-digit number that, when multiplied by 4, equals 34, 64 or 94. 34 and 94 are not divisible by 4 so it must be 64. The middle two digits must be 1 and 6, as $4 \times 16 = 64$.

The code is 4 2 1 6 6 4 and the fourth digit is 6.

25 Both Felix's and Olivia's reasoning is correct. Felix is correct because if the size scores were different but the scores for taste were the same, then their final scores could not be equal. Olivia is correct because if the scores for size were the same but the scores for taste were different, then their final scores could not be equal.

The other options are incorrect by a process of elimination.

26 As all the statements are incorrect, the blue counters don't belong to Billy, Patrick or Henry. So Elijah has the blue counters. The red counters don't belong to Billy or Henry, nor do they belong to Elijah. So Patrick has the red counters. Henry doesn't have the blue or red counters and he doesn't have green. Henry must have the yellow counters. Billy has the remaining colour: green.

27 The gym owner claims that naming the dog park after a poppy would be insulting to servicemen and women because the red poppy is a symbol of their sacrifice. The statement that the RSL proposed the name **most** weakens this claim because the RSL represents returned servicemen and women so if they proposed the

name themselves, they must not find it insulting.

A and B are incorrect. These statements about the meaning of the purple poppy provide background information about why the name Purple Poppy Dog Park was proposed. They strengthen the proposal for the new name and weaken the gym owner's claim—but they do not **most** weaken the claim.

C is incorrect. This statement neither strengthens nor weakens the claim.

28 All of the shapes can be made with the three pieces of card.

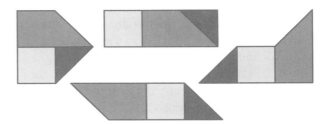

29 There are 6 symbols for one of the sectors. It is not the greatest or least number of symbols so that sector is not East or South. If it represented North, then 6 symbols would represent 30 birds and 1 symbol would represent 5 birds. Seven symbols would represent 7×5 or 35 birds, which is more than any sector in the table. The 6 symbols cannot represent North.

So 6 symbols must represent West and 24 birds. $24 \div 6 = 4$ so each symbol represents 4 birds. Half a symbol would represent 2 birds.

$7\frac{1}{2}$ symbols would represent $7 \times 4 + 2$ or 30 birds, which is the number for North.

$5\frac{1}{2}$ symbols would represent $5 \times 4 + 2$ or 22 birds, which is the number for South. The sector that must still be drawn is East.

30 We know that any volunteers who did not have a chance to work in the penguin enclosure on the last roster **will** be chosen to work in the penguin enclosure on the next roster. However, this does not mean that anyone who worked there on the last roster will definitely **not** be chosen to work there again on the next roster.

So this sentence shows the flaw in Bree's reasoning and she may still be able to work in the penguin enclosure on the next roster.

A and C are incorrect. These sentences are true and are not mistakes Bree has made.

D is incorrect. This sentence is a mistake since the supervisor said they **definitely will** be given a chance to work there on the next roster. However, it is not a mistake Bree has made.

31 Each shape must be a mirror image of each shape that it is next to, where the fold is the line of symmetry. In A the top two shapes are mirrored (as are the bottom two) but the left two are not (and nor are the right two). In B none of the adjacent shapes are mirror images of each other. In C the left two shapes are mirror images of each other (as are the right two) but the top two are not (and nor are the bottom two). In D each shape is the mirror image of the two shapes it is adjacent to.

32 Since Logan was in the Writing Club, the spelling and grammar score was not relevant in his case. Logan's story only had to be within the word-count limit to be selected. Since his story was not selected, it must have been outside the word-count limit.

A is incorrect. This statement might be true. However, since Logan was in the Writing Club, the spelling and grammar score was not relevant in his case. So it cannot be the reason that his story was not selected.

C is incorrect. The information tells us that Logan was in the Writing Club.

D is incorrect. Since Logan was in the Writing Club, the preferred topic list was not relevant in his case. So this cannot be the reason that his story was not selected.

33 The first three people are seated easily, as shown in the diagram below. After Camilla sits, the next empty seat is passed and Diana sits between Albie and Bertie. Then the next empty seat is passed and Eddie sits between Albie and Camilla, directly on Albie's right.

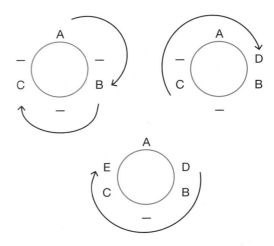

34 If the scissors are next to the green box, we must find out where that box is.

The white box is farthest left and the pink box is next to it. The blue box is 3 spaces away from the pink so must be the farthest right. The red box is 2 spaces from the blue so must be in the middle of the row and the green box must go into the only spot left, second on the right. If the scissors are next to the green box, but not in the middle, they must be in the blue box, which is farthest to the right.

| White | Pink | Red | Green | Blue |

35 The nutritionist's argument is that microgreens (tiny baby vegetables) activate powerful antioxidants and are the most nutritious foods you can eat to boost your immune system. The fact that microgreens produce 100 times more antioxidants than mature vegetables strengthens this argument.

A is incorrect. This statement adds to the information about vegetables being important to the production of antioxidants but does not strengthen the nutritionist's claim about microgreens.

C is incorrect. This statement summarises the nutritionist's argument.

D is incorrect. This restates a comment already made by the nutritionist and so does not add to the argument.

36 Train A is halfway between Sydney and Newcastle at 2 pm when Train B starts its journey. Because Train B is only half as fast as Train A, it will only cover half the distance in the same time. Train A will cover two-thirds of the remaining distance in two-thirds of an hour, which is 40 minutes. Train B will cover only half that distance in 40 minutes. The trains will pass each other at 2:40 pm.

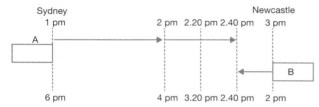

37 Eight cows have twins (16 calves).

As 98 − 16 = 82, the remaining 154 cows have 82 calves. 154 − 82 = 72 so 72 cows do not have a calf.

38 The person who is first in line has the green bag so is not Luisa. Both Chung and Lily are behind others so cannot be first. Isaac must be the person who is first and who has the green bag and buys milk. Neither Luisa nor Lily has the red bag so that person must be Chung. So Lily is directly behind Chung. Chung is directly in front of the person buying eggs so that is Lily. Luisa is not buying meat, nor is she buying milk or eggs. Luisa must be buying bread.

39 Alice is correct because if the only invertebrates that have wings are insects, then an animal with wings that isn't an insect cannot be an invertebrate.

B is incorrect. Just because the only invertebrates that have wings are insects, it does not follow that any invertebrate that does not have wings is not an insect.

C and D are incorrect by a process of elimination.

40 To come to the conclusion that four entrants will get prizes, Eman has added the one special prize to the three prizes for first, second and third. He has then assumed that the four prizes will go to four different students. He has not considered that the special prizewinner might also come first, second or third—and therefore will receive two of the prizes. Therefore it is possible for only three entrants to get prizes.

A is incorrect. The information tells us that each entrant can enter only one painting in the competition. So this sentence shows a mistake; however, it is not a mistake Eman has made.

B and C are incorrect. These statements might be true but they do not impact the number of prizes and they are not mistakes Eman has made.

NOTES